ECONOMIC PROGRESS AND SOCIAL JUSTICE

TOWARDS SOCIAL SECTOR DEVELOPMENT

Dedicated to

the memory of

Dr. D.S. Awasthi

former President IEA

Contents

Preface

The development economists and policy-makers are unanimous in their view that the development of social sector is most crucial for accelerated economic development with adequate emphasis on social justice. It has been seen from all development experience of various countries in the world that those who have ignored the development of social sector have done so at the risk of adversely affecting the economic progress and social justice. It is vitally recognised that the social sector is the most fundamental prerequisite for the progress of a country.

Social sector—the backbone of development has assumed immense significance in India in the past decades. The core view is that it provides enhanced capabilities for a nation's manpower to tread the path of economic growth, although governmental outlay on its various spheres e.g. education in service, training, health, nutrition and income levels—where self-investment leads to boundless human capital formation—is almost negligible, thereby thwarting any endeavours for an accessible growth-oriented economic headway. As a logical sequence to the pursuit of this approach, the social arena is fast losing its potentiality.

Nevertheless, the spurring issue in the 1990s has been the sustained focus by UNDP (United Nation's Development Programme) on social attainments conforming to the ideals of equity, growth and social justice. This is to be imperatively realised by our policy-makers coupled with streamlined implementation so as to facilitate the progress of economic reformation.

On the eve of golden jubilee celebration by our Parliament,

a modest and inspiring resolution was adopted for universalisation of primary education by 2000 AD, and also need-marking the importance of health-care facilities for infrastructural stronghold. In economic parlance our demoralised society first needs to rid itself from the shackles of those factors which contribute to erosion of equity and social justice in an economy. It is in this context that the role of human capital in socio-economic development is exigent for the pursuance of economic reforms process.

In this book both the micro as well as the macro approach has been perceptibly undertaken in several papers—which elaborate on the expanding role and contribution of human resources in strengthening the social sector. A committed attempt has been made to study the lacuna, problems and implications of this sector's performance along with remedies and suggestions in this regard.

According to Dr. D.S. Awasthi, generation of social equity and justice demands substantial efforts by a nation towards a welfare-oriented economy to boost the process of economic reforms. In this respect, protection and preservation of human capital need special mention—the focal stress point being a healthy and educated labour personnel. A fact of vital significance is that such human resource would not merely accelerate development but also, as a prerequisite, serve as a powerful tool of equity generation for fulfilling the objectives laid down by this sector. Dr. B.M. Jani, tries to sort out issues and policy options for medical care expenditure. Health and Medical service is one of the important segments of service sector in India. There is always a controversy among economists that free or highly subsidised social service like health-care service have not led to adequate access for the poor. He suggested, pricing policy for health services should aim, resource mobilisation, promotion of efficiency and equity too. As a part of insurance sector reform, entry of private sector and foreign insurance companies encouraged for better health-care insurance service through competitive insurance market.

Dr. A.D.N. Bajpai opines that the social sector development is not merely a social necessity but also an economic essentiality and above all a political compulsion. The government has been investing resources for the development of these sectors but the results are not noteworthy due to insufficiency of resources and improper, inefficient and ineffective utilisation of resources. Though private sector's involvement in social sector development is being advocated but its commitment to the cause is doubtful. So is the case with NGO's. Hence, in the democratic setup like ours no government can afford to neglect social sector in long-run. Dr. Narendra Prasad in his paper finds that it is impossible to assure a steady flow of required manpower for a modern economy unless a huge educational super structure is build up in India. It is, therefore, imperative for developing countries like ours to put greater emphasis on human capital investment through investment in education because "By sowing seed, you will harvest once, By planting a tree, you will harvest ten-fold, By educating the people, you will harvest one hundred-fold". Dr. P.C. Tiwari discusses and evaluates the role of people's participation in development planning which is still nebulous by concept and inappropriately defined in government plans. To attain positive returns as a measure of effective implementation, it need to be ensured that the terms 'bureaucracy' and 'government' aren't synonymous as also democratic and responsible decentralisation be distinctively achieved.

Dr. V.P. Tripathi and Dr. Diwakar Khare in an analytical study of bonded labour suggested that mere release of the bonded persons is not necessary. The eradication or rehabilitation programmes must see that the economic rehabilitation and value orientation is properly attempted and ensured. Otherwise, even a good-intentioned welfare legislation may prove futile and abortive and it may potentially intensify the bondage and suffering of the poor. Moreover, there is an urgent need to change the attitudes of the people i.e., employers as well as employees.

Dr. T.K. Jha has evaluated Indian women as the backbone of the family. The society can't go ahead in lack of women education. To educate a woman means to educate the whole family. Only an educated woman can fulfil the all-round development of her children, thus she might lay the strong foundation of her offspring. Therefore, the education of women means to educate the coming generation of our country. Hence, for economic and social progress of the country there is a great need of project education of women. Dr. T.C. Pathak opines that the expansion of social sector in India has brought about changes in the human resource through its impact on size and quality of population, but because of increase in population, rise in per capita income is not very high and poverty ratio though reduced is still high. Similarly, expansion of education has raised literacy ratio but also created the problem of educated unemployment causing frustration among the youth. Hence, there is a need of complete change in the outlook of the people so that to remove adverse effects of social sector expansion and to achieve high growth rate by the economy.

Dr. Pratima Trivedi views that social welfare calls for higher investment in Human Resource Development so as to strengthen the country's social sector. It is the human capital which contributes towards the co-existence of physical and social progress if considerable heed is imparted to education and health—the pillars of economic development. Dr. Mukul Srivastava conceptualises the rapidly growing significance of egalitarian planning which is indispensable for reforming our economy. A feasible economic and social development strategy be devised containing not merely rising income levels but also promotion of social justice (distributive) in developing economies like India. Dr. Harshada S. Rathod, tried to make the picture of Health and Education, clear among SAARC countries. She concluded that SAARC countries need more money to continue improving the quality of basic education. She suggested that special programmes for making the adults, meaningfully literate should be given high priority, so that the efforts of the Human Development Resources for their children are not adversely affected. Moreover, SAARC cannot be viewed as the panacea to all the problems that South Asian countries have accumulated for themselves over the decades.

Mr. Satyendraji Srivastava, suggested that the wave of privatisation, liberalisation and globalisation should not be allowed to enter into the realm of human development.

Competition in this area would mean a monstrous denial of the fundamental rights guaranteed to a citizen in the Indian Constitution. Government at all levels, should be particular to realise the catastrophe of deprivation as both health and education services are going beyond the reach of a common man. There should be no compromise on the point of extending equal opportunity for human development to one and all and obliterate the duality from health and education services. Dr. V.P. Tripathi and Dr. Virendra Prakash in their study find that after 1990 the economic scenario has changed owing to new economic reforms, i.e. economic reforms in HRD. But public sector alone cannot take up the challenge of its own. The future of Human Resource Development (HRD) therefore lies in the hands of private sector. They concluded to say that new generation have to be well equipped to have their proper place in market economy, we can, therefore, look forward a day when market mechanism and monetary motivations will successfully manage human resource development what planning system failed to do.

Dr. Mukulika Hitkari opines that development of economy with its reform process manifests itself solely in the infrastructural thrust. Commitment requires improvement in the state of Human capital so as to perpetuate an egalitarian vision of society. In other words, human development aspect—health at the centre stage—requires its integration with the provision of social services.

Dr. O.P. Shukla observes that the social sector development in any economy has a vital role to pay. It has a direct bearing upon HRD. The long-term goals depend upon this aspect. During the pre-reform period, in this direction, public policy was understood as a major instrument. In post-reform period, seven years down the road from 1991, the sketchy impact shows a diverse trend. However, the need of the hour, to suggest, is to have a participatory approach comprising both market and public, for social sector development.

I owe a great deal of gratitude to all the contributors of this volume who have taken great pains in preparing their articles covering various aspects of the subject. I sincerely thank Dr. D.S. Awasthi, Director, Development Studies Academy,

Kanpur and ex-President, Indian Economic Association (IEA), who has guided the preparation of this volume and also in persuading the various contributors to send their article for this volume. I am also thankful to Dr. Mukulika Hitkari, Senior Lecturer, D.G. College, Kanpur, who has extended all possible help and cooperation in preparing the manuscript and getting it ready for the press. I also express my heartfelt gratitude to Mr. V.D. Trivedi, Income-Tax Commissioner, New Delhi, for his valuable help by shouldering the total responsibility of publishing this volume.

Furthermore, I ardently hope that the ideas and views as expressed by the contributors in their respective papers would by valuably imformative for development in the social sector arena.

Finally, I am thankful to Deep & Deep Publications Pvt. Ltd., for publishing this book in stimulated period and in most impressive form.

Kanpur PRATIMA TRIVEDI

List of Contributors

Awasthi, D.S., Director, Development Studies Academy, Kanpur and ex-President, Indian Economic Association.

Bajpai, A.D.N., Reader and Head, Department of Post-Graduate Studies and Research in Economics, R.D. University, Jabalpur (M.P.).

Hitkari, Mukulika, Senior Lecturer, Department of Economics, D.G. Post-Graduate College, Kanpur, U.P.

Jani, B.M., Department of Economics, Saurashtra University, Rajkot, Gujarat.

Jha, T.K., Reader in Economics, University Department, L.N.M. University, Darbhanga, Bihar.

Khare, Diwakar, Reader, Department of Statistics, Institute of Social Sciences, Dr. B.R. Ambedkar University, Agra, U.P.

Pathak, T.C., Formerly, Head of Economics Department, Government College, Ajmer, and Retd. Principal.

Prakash, Virendra, Asstt. Professor in Economics, Government Post-Graduate College, Morena, M.P.

Prasad, Narendra, Professor of Economics, Magadh University, Bodhgaya, Bihar.

Rathod, Harshada S., Department of Economics, Smt. P.N. Doshi Women's College, Ghatkopar, Mumbai.

Shukla, O.P., Lecturer, Department of Economics, Armapore P.G. College, Armapore, Kanpur, U.P.

Srivastava, Mukul, Lecturer, Department of Social Work, Institute of Social Sciences, Agra, U.P.

Srivastava, S.J., Senior Lecturer, Department of Economics, D.B.S. College, Kanpur, U.P.

Tiwari, P.C., Reader, Department of Economics, Handia Post-Graduate College, Handia, Allahabad, U.P.

Tripathi, V.P., Reader in Economics, Department, R.B.S. College, Agra, U.P.

Trivedi, Pratima, Head, Department of Economics, Guru Nanak Girls' Post-Graduate College, Kanpur, U.P.

1

Inequitable and Imbalance Social Sector Development and its Impact on Economic Development in India

D.S. AWASTHI*

The economists and development strategists are of the unanimous view that adequate and balanced social sector development is vitally important for just and equitable economic development of the country. The material resources and capital accumulation is helpful for accelerating economic development but more important is the social sector development. Social sector in underdeveloped countries is of vital importance and is considered fundamental to fundamental or basic to basic requirements of economic development. In those countries where social sector has not been given adequate importance we have seen the adverse effect on economic growth. We will discuss this aspect in the Indian context in the following pages.

The ultimate objective of all human endeavour is the attainment of happiness and welfare. It is rightly acknowledged that the true parameter of development is removal of poverty,

* Director, Development Studies Academy, Kanpur and ex-President, Indian Economic Association.

unemployment and inequality. The success of development efforts is expressed in terms of our capacity 'to wipe out tears from the eyes of the poor' or 'to bring smile on the face of the common man' or to achieve economic development with 'human face'. In special circumstances there may be evaluation of our performance in terms of improvement in balance of payment, preservation of adequate foreign exchange reserves, satisfactory export performance and stability of exchange rate. But in view of our limited role in foreign sector as indicated by our less than one percent share in international trade, we have to largely concentrate on our efforts on domestic front for reducing the percentage of population below the poverty line, improving the living standard of people in terms of greater availability of essential things of life, removing unemployment, reducing concentration of economic power removal of regional disparities and improving the quality of human capital in terms of better health and education.

With political freedom in 1947 one phase of our historic struggle came to an end and the new one for economic freedom began. It was expected that our new freedom will redeem millions of people from the bondage of poverty, unemployment, inequality, backwardness and exploitation. But even after fifty years of independence we have failed in achieving our goal of equity and social justice. We have repeatedly affirmed our faith in these objectives and expressed our dedication for making efforts in this direction but subversive forces have frustrated our efforts.

We have not been able to reduce income disparities as lowest 10% people have 3.70% income and the lowest 20% people have share of 8.5% income and top 200% people have 42.60% of income and highest 100% people have 28.4% income. This inequitable distribution pattern even compares unfavourably to the rich countries like U.S.A., Germany and Japan where corresponding concentration figures are marginally smaller. In terms of one $ per day PPP based poverty comparable ratio India has 52.5% poor population while the corresponding figures for China is 29.4%. In the world there are only about a dozen countries whose poverty ratio is higher than India. In terms of H.D.I. 1996 ranks, there are 134 countries which are having better performance than us. We have adopted the globalization policy in the context of the world with vast disparities. The rich and poor countries income gap is very wide. Indian per capita income is $ 340 while that of China is $ 620. Low income countries average income is $ 430 as against the World average of $ 4880. The rich countries' per capita incomes are very high, like U.S.A. $ 26980 and Japan $ 39640 and Germany $ 27510. In the present context of iniquitous world, there exist fundamental differences of interest and circumstances.

Our difficulties are complex in view of our market-oriented reforms on one hand and coexisting massive poverty, unemployment and exploitation on the other, also we have to protect the interests of equity, social justice and harmony. Market-oriented economic policies cannot adequately respond to the challenges of fundamental issues of our economy including eradication of poverty and unemployment, conservation of environment, removal of concentration of economic power, provision of uniform and standard education and other welfare programmes.

If we look back to the fifty years of freedom there are many achievements in the fields of science and technology, agricultural production, life expectancy, industrial and infrastructure development along with expansion of social services. But as regards socio-economic equality, balanced regional development and improvement in human capital, our performance has been disappointing. Here we will try to examine some aspects of erosion of equity and social justice in our development process.

SOCIAL SECTORS AND INEQUITY GENERATION

Human capital is a fundamental prerequisite to economic development with social justice. In poor developing countries the preservation and protection of human capital is of vital importance. Healthy, educated, trained, motivated and dedicated manpower will not only accelerate development process but will also make it equitable and just. Such human resource will have an inbuilt mechanism to resist the forces of exploitation and combat the inequity generating mechanism of vested interests. Healthy and educated manpower will surely help in providing the millions of people relief from poverty, unemployment and suffering. It needs to be examined how these new economic reforms motivated by considerations of efficiency, productivity, cost minimisation, international market constraints along with new organisational set up of multinational corporations/agencies dictated by goals of profit maximisation would protect the objectives of equity and social justice in a country like India with mass illiteracy, poor health standards, surplus labour obsolete production techniques, duality of educational structure, limited and inequitable facilities of management/technical education, etc. There is general well substantiated impression that the new growth strategy in special circumstances might have registered higher growth rate, better export performance, a liberalised trade atmosphere generating greater profit opportunities or comfortable foreign currency reserves but on equity and social justice front the performance is dismal and has created social and economic tensions. While it needs to be examined in greater depth the fact that transition to new economic reforms produced disquieting developments in few cases. Russian experience of reforms in terms of falling of life expectancy between 1990-94, increase in mortality in older age group due to cardio-vascular diseases and in younger group due to accidents, suicide, drug abuse, murder and similar indications. It is admitted that direct cause to these unfortunate and painful developments needs more investigation but there is indirect evidence linking this with economic hard ships, declining quality of life and access to medical care are also linked with the situation. This further indicates causal link between declining living conditions, increased stresses and strains, alcohol consumption and inefficiency in law enforcement agencies. The worsening of employment situation as a result of reform measures has created painful development situation. In China, ten million people lost jobs due to closure in public enterprises out of which only four million could be absorbed under various schemes of re-employment. The modernisation process adopted in many countries ultimately resulted in labour surplus situation. In many countries this shock was absorbed in view of many satisfactory re-employment, unemployment guarantee and compensation schemes. The position in India is entirely different.

With adoption of new economic reforms a general impression is firmly gaining ground that our country's commitment to welfare state has become questionable. The objective of welfare of the poor and the interests of the market are often irreconcilable.

INDIAN EDUCATION SYSTEM AND PERPETUATION OF INEQUITIES

It is reasonably expected that inequities and disparities in the growth process could largely be corrected by spread of education, improvement in health and employment creation programmes for weak and deprived. It has been observed that the social sector development has not proved to be an effective instrument in removing social inequalities and exploitation. Instead of promoting equity and harmony these are proving to be instruments of perpetuating inequalities in the society.

Education system can serve the goal of establishing a just social order, emancipating the society from the clutches of poverty, exploitation, discrimination and generate feelings of brotherhood, infuse the spirit of dedication and sacrifice for the society to raise the levels of productivity and efficiency and to dismantle the barriers of discrimination of sex, caste, region, religion etc. It is a painful fact that the Indian investment on education is inadequate. Central government expenditure on education during 1981-90 and 1991-95 was 2.2% and 2% of GNP respectively while in the corresponding period such investment in Sri Lanka was 8.60% and 10.20%, in Ghana 21% and 23.40% and in Zambia 9% and 12.80%. In our case not only allocation is inadequate but its utilisation is also poor and unsatisfactory.

In India, the most shocking and painful reality is that education has helped in perpetuating inequalities and disparities. The Indian education system from the primary to highest level is designed separately for the rich and the poor, which only assists in widening the social disparities and economic inequalities. India has the availability of export quality education imparted to less than 1 percent privileged people through excellent centres of education and sub-standard, spurious education rendered through Institutions controlled by private individuals, profiteers and racketeers available to the rest 99 percent people.

The process of social inequity is generated from the primary education. There, in some public schools children pay fee more than per capita income of the country and the educational facilities and amenities provided are comparable to the best in the world. In sharp contrast to these schools there are primary schools in rural areas, where even the lowest standard of education is not maintained. Whatever be the achievements propagated about these schools they are largely false and fabricated. Innumerable surprise inspection reports have shown that these schools are often found closed teachers either absent or partly present and the facilities are scanty. The seeds of inequality and injustice are engrained in the tender minds of children and the parents grow under sensitivity of the injustice of the duality of this iniquitous education system. The most tragic part of the story is that there is dismal performance of our state in checking and controlling this inequitable process.

The duality of education would accentuate the social and economic inequalities. The process of inequitable educational growth has further received impetus under the present privatisation policy of the government. The propagators of market-oriented growth policies and international agencies advocating reforms are probably either ignorant or indifferent to the ground realities of the education. It is expected that the inequities of the market-oriented system may partly be cured by proper investment on human capital in terms of well educated and trained manpower. In a country like India the situation is complicated where educational disparities have contributed to further accentuation of the disparities in income distribution and earning capabilities of the weaker sections of the society.

The condition of education at different levels including technical and management education further exhibit the chaotic and unequal dispensation of resource to the different categories of institutions. There are pure state sector institutions like universities I.I.Ts., management institutes, government colleges along with government-aided private institutions and pure private educational institutions. In the situation of increasing population and demand for educational institutions and growing resource constraints and limitation of the state to respond the government gave an opportunity to the private managements to run and manage the educational institutions. The control of the government and universities, through Acts and Ordinances proved to be only formal and ritualistic. Educational authorities were mostly collusive parties to massive conspiracy to operate the system for their private monetary gains.

It was contemplated that the scheme of self-financing will satisfy the interests of all concerned. Private managements often dominated by politicians, desiring to earn fabulous income and wealth free from any encumbrances or tax liability. It will be interesting to know that a large number of members of legislative bodies run and manage these institutions directly or remotely. This protects their political interests and economic gains. Innocent and ignorant people are happy about the expansion of educational facility regardless of its being irrelevant and sub-standard, the government is happy that it is arranging the supply of education facility without incurring any financial liability and the political proponents of privatisation are happy that the objective is being fulfilled.

In many such institutions policy of extortion is practised which creates social tensions. The society does not know that non-marketable bogus education is imparted and often the corrupt practices like mass copying are encouraged as there are no teachers to teach or they are fraudulently shown on the records to reimburse money from the government, in case non-aided institutions are taken over by the government. In a state when the High Court intervened and ordered the check on mass copying though state machinery the results came down from 60% to 80%. What could be more shocking state of the affairs in real education world? The teachers in that state paraded before authorities to inform that they have not been paid salary for the period extending to a year in many cases. One wonders as to how these people were surviving without any payment? The answer is obvious that they were having some other source of income like undertaking private coaching. Barring the teachers who are paid salary from government and are highly unionised the job insecurity and practice of underpayment is widely prevalent. This is also directly affecting the weaker and poor sections of the society. The education system is developing signs of inequity and disparity generation at all levels and there have been no effective measures taken to check these unhealthy developments.

In conclusion, it can be said that the system of education in our country and its post-independence growth has not served the cause of equity and social justice. This is a painful reality in our case that education which is supposed to be the most powerful tool for achieving equity and social justice has been so conspired and has produced inequitable consequences and widened the gap between the rich and the poor.

HEALTH SERVICES AND INEQUITABLE DISPENSATION

The other area of social service which is expected to contribute to growth and social justice is health. In our country, investment on health is inadequate. The central government expenditure on health during 1981-90 and 1991-95 was only 2% of the GNP while in countries like Ghana it was 8.5% and 7.8%, Zambia 6.5% and 9.9% and in Sri Lanka 4.7% and 5.5%. Investment in health facilities for poor and weaker class is of paramount importance. Improvement in health standards especially of productive labour class is directly linked with the economic productivity. Poor health conditions in a country like India are directly linked to poverty. There should be equal attention to increase in the investment and proper utilisation of the same. Unfortunately, the expenditure marked for the health services for the poor sections of the society has been siphoned-off. The recent example of medical scam only touch the tip of the iceberg. Since the advent of privatisation policies, health facilities comparable to developed countries are fast emerging, of which many of them have been financed by public resources. But their extremely expensive character has deprived the poor of these services. The real picture about dispensation of health services is very painful, acquisitive and a materialistic wave is sweeping the scenario.

This has resulted in opening of nursing homes of different categories. The competitive parallel private medical structure is gradually dismantling the existing public hospitals and continuing to erode people's confidence in public health system. The poor people are persuaded rather coerced to take admission to these hospitals and spend their life time savings to save the lives of near and dear ones. The survey of the present arrangements expose the nefarious designs of many unethical members of the medical profession. The public doctors attend hospitals to recruit patients for nursing homes. The government of this poor country make payment of salaries to these doctors while, their services are rendered in private nursing homes. Premier hospitals with overcrowded wards in the past are empty today, thanks to the new scheme of transfer of patients from public hospitals to private nursing homes. Only those patients are left there, who cannot afford to move and are compelled to buy the treatment in these hospitals. With these arrangements one can expect how public health schemes are responding to the challenges of the market economy on one hand and our commitment to equity and social justice on the other. In hospitals situated in rural and semi-urban areas, the conditions are pitiable. There may be exceptions but these observations amply expose the realities of medical and health service conditions in our country.

WELFARE AND EMPLOYMENT GENERATING PROGRAMMES

The massive leakage of resources from the allocation of welfare programmes have further created inequities. The well organised intermediaries, vested interests and administrative agencies take the lions' share of these schemes. We would like to comment on the employment situation as witnessed by us. Under the present era of new economic reforms and international competitive environment, employment might be created in certain highly profitable and competitively advantaged sectors but the situation is so frustrating and demoralising in other sectors. Kanpur is a big metropolitan town with 4 million population and was once known in the country and outside as the Manchester of the East. There were many textile mills employing a large labour force. Today, all 11 mills are closed rendering the labour force surplus. Many schemes of their modernisation and revival were evolved. Gradually sizeable labour force has been eased out under exit schemes and the remaining labour force is being paid for years without any work. This is a pathetic condition of employment and the present reform programmes could not bring traditional industries to life. The labour force rendered surplus has absorbed itself in unorganised/informal sector segments or have migrated back to rural areas. There is no authentic information about such a large labour force disappearance. We are concentrating on development aspect without much attention paid to human hardships and inequity consequences.

The menace of sickness of small scale industries also give very painful revelations. With the motive of grabbing loans many unscrupulous elements establish these enterprises and after extracting out funds render them sick thus causing serious financial losses to agencies. The results of working of these agencies at the same time expose the hollow claims of preservation of social justice and equity. The one inescapable conclusion of all these studies is that the vital questions of health, welfare and education in a country with a large population comprising millions of poor people and rampant corruption should not be left to the mercy of market forces. There is a need more than before, to have a more dominant participation, efficient regulation and stricter control of the state. It is rather unfortunate that wrong conclusions have been drawn from past experience. The objective of social equity and justice was subverted by weak and unfair implementation of the regulation and not the regulations as such. The vested interests and Mafia groups on one hand adopted double strategy of creating hurdles in the execution of regulations and making them ineffective and on the other hand advocating about their futility, thus creating an atmosphere of fully unchecked misuse of power to exploit the weaker sections of the society.

DEMONSTRATIVE CONSUMERISM VERSUS MASS SUB-STANDARD LIVING CONDITIONS

With growth of income and wealth disparities, there has been a spurt in demonstrative consumerism and indulgence in luxurious living. With the advent of liberalisation and globalization process the phenomenon of demonstrative consumerism has assumed alarming proportions. All possible help to new investors and business class, both of foreign and national origin is provided in the present system. The experts saw in India a huge market of all types of luxury products. A highly competitive market in automobiles and consumer durables developed as the manufacturers and investors thought that sufficient demand has been created as the rich class will consume all these products. The massive investment on aggressive advertising is reflective of this new phenomenon.

There is a paradoxical situation generated by inequitable development pattern. On one hand there is vast majority of people who are denied basic essentials of life facing acute shortage either due to non-availability of products or lack of purchasing power and on the other there is excessive supply of unwarranted luxury items. Many multinational corporations and joint ventures have identified this newly rich people as their target group. Many recent policies not only have facilitated inequitable concentration of resources but has also helped in their retention through liberal fiscal treatment.

The process of liberalisation and globalization has created an unjust situation of unwarranted production of luxury goods for which there was lack of sustained demand of such products with consequent recession. A country which professes highest noble intentions of protecting the objectives of equity and social justice has to warrant resources for removal of recession in luxury goods meant to cater the needs of the rich consumers. The market-oriented system would lead to emergence of such crisis which can hardly be justified in the economic conditions of poor countries like ours. The precious national resources going in for production of luxurious consumer durables under compulsive competitive conditions may give temporary laugh to a certain section of consumers at the cost of waste of precious scarce national resources, which if invested in growth of infrastructure and other essential sectors of economy would have helped us in fighting war against poverty. If under the dictates of market and high profit expectations certain multinational corporations producing luxury goods generate disequilibrium of excessive supply, then the consequences of the same should be borne by them. If the state had to intervene it should have done at the stage where such imprudent decisions were taken. We should have a clean slate policy of charting the growth process which is equitable and socially just. Those who have created recession should suffer its consequences.

The wasteful indulgence in luxurious living has other inequitable consequences. If the earnings are diverted to the implementation of social health and education programmes it could have reduced social tensions. The damage caused to productive power of the country as a result of this frustration should be properly imputed. These real economic issues on which if serious attention is not paid at early stages the volcanic eruptions will submerge peace and stability of the country.

It is interesting to see how some analysts thought that the recession would partly be remedied by the extra purchasing power generated by disbursement of Rs. 5100 crores to the employees on the recommendation of the Fifth Pay Commission. Those who were opposing such payments and considered them inflationary and deficit generating were seeing in it the germs of recovery.

We should not fail to analyse the linkages between demonstrative consumerism, diversion of resources to production of luxury goods, short-term high profit, entry of many firms lured by the possibilities of a vast market, highly aggressive westernised advertising campaigns, disappearance of short-term boom conditions, emergence of recessionary conditions, clamour for state intervention in terms of further liberalisation, reduction in interest rates and more liquidity and availability of resources in unwarranted production activities. While lowering down of interest rates might give temporary relief to a few involved in production of luxury goods it does cause hardships to a large number of small investors and pensioners whose income is confined to the saving deposited in banking institutions. This relationship channel is getting well exposed to the masses in spite of their illiteracy and ignorance.

India professed Gandhian philosophy and adherence to its teaching of simple living and highest priority for welfare of the weakest. India has been claiming leadership of weak and poor countries. By the present trend of indulgence in luxurious living by rich and consequent growth of disparities, we are definitely losing our grounds for moral leadership. The erosion of our values is amply demonstrated in mass advertising campaigns it will definitely have adverse effects. It would be most appropriate to emphasize that the fundamental strength of Indian economy is its people, if freed from bondage of exploitation, injustice, frustration, social divisions and is motivated, spirited, educated, trained and armed with a sacrificing temperament. It is most unfortunate that this aspect has not been given the priority which it deserved most. Any survey of people on the issues of their morale, objectives of the policy and the character of policy-makers and rulers will have the most shocking revelations. People in general are losing faith and they are growing indifferent to the system. Their tension and frustrations are mounting though it is not canalised in a mass movement or struggle because of clever mechanisation to divide them on the bases of caste, religion and region. These short-term diversions would ultimately fail to distract the minds of the people from the real issues in the long-run.

CRIMINAL NEXUS BETWEEN BUSINESS MAFIA, POLITICIANS AND BUREAUCRACY

For equitable growth and, social justice a state committed to welfare doctrine armed with constitutional authority are of paramount importance. A welfare State should be capable of providing good governance. Good governance is reflected by qualities of accountability, transparency, integrity, efficiency, impartiality and above all sensitivity to the suffering of the people. On the spectrum of governance evaluation this varies from good, average and bad with exceptional instances of excellent and worst. Our standard of governance is unfortunately very unsatisfactory. The standard differences relate to the level of governmental working and administration. At the highest level it is very efficient, sophisticated, well organised and comprehensive, comparable to the best in the world. The most efficient technical and trained manpower is employed at the higher level. But as we go below the scale its quality deteriorates and there is interference and corruption. This is particularly relevant with regard to the schemes of welfare and equity relating to poverty eradication, employment generation, primary education, health and welfare of tribal and Harijan communities. There may be some areas of development where satisfactory system of inspection, evaluation and monitoring exist but in case of welfare programmes the implementation and governance is extremely unsatisfactory. The nexus between rich vested interests, powerful politicians, strong Mafia groups corrupt bureaucracy and government machinery is impregnable. Unfortunately this nexus has been becoming strong and powerful over the period of time.

The criminal elements have now sizeable domination and influence over our legislative structure. The Election Commission in a recent disclosure indicated the extent to which law-breakers have become law-makers. Out of 4227 M.L.A.'s in the country 700 were involved in criminal cases and in the recent elections, out of 13,592 candidates there were 1,500 candidates had criminal record of all descriptions.

The system of governance had been degenerating within the present constitutional apparatus. At no stage the powerful organs of the state, which were still safe, did intervene in the process to arrest the trend of demoralisation set in under which independent and honest working of administration was made difficult. The highest cadres of administrative and police services did not remain servant of the state but had come to be known to be attached to political individuals. The political interference and degeneration of the machinery of governance has increased. In Uttar Pradesh, during the period—July 1991 and May 1997 there were five Chief Ministers/Governors under President rule and in each five cases there were massive transfers 1-I.A.S. 293, I.P.S. 228, 2-I.A.S. 321, I.P.S. 493, 3-I.A.S. 329, I.P.S. 283, 4-I.A.S., 163, I.P.S. 151, 5-I.A.S. 181 and I.P.S. 229. There is an urgent need to estimate the economic consequences of the instable political process.

The relation between criminal nexus and the authority have witnessed four stages over the time. First, criminal elements' influence was marginal; Second, criminal elements' greater emergence and the state exercised weakened control; Third, the criminal and Mafia elements developed powerful domination while the state became tolerant and collusive; Fourth, strong dominating relationship of criminal elements became apparent and state machinery started working on the dictates of criminal elements. Criminal elements assumed authority through democratic process. The bureaucracy gradually got demoralised and honest elements frustrate while the corrupt ones get premium and rewards. The Vohra Committee Report has well established this conclusion. The conclusions are generalised rather than with pointed references to enable the action to be initiated. The judiciary is making efforts to protect the rights of citizens in implementation of welfare programmes without corruption. In a democratic constitutional set up people have a right to be governed judiciously and protected from unwarranted interferences and discrimination. The Supreme Court and High Courts are not only checking and preventing this nexus but are also monitoring and administering the impartial investigations and protecting the agencies from the interferences of the vested interests. It is unfortunate that in view of failures of administrative agencies the highest judicial organs are performing the administrative functions inspite of all limitations. World Development Report 1997 also makes reference to the political interference and demoralisation of bureaucracy in India.

In our system the formal situations are far different from informal arrangements. Visible apparent systems are different from invisible and informal systems. This makes the issues of distortions and misappropriation very apt. Ideological pretensions are very different from realistic ground level operations. We can very well imagine that under this context how the policies of welfare measures can successfully be implemented. This should be understood that under the present convertibility mechanisms, different types of power get transformed into each other according to demands of the situation, like muscle power into political power, administrative and political power into material power and so on.

EQUITY SUBVERSION—POLITICAL AND ECONOMIC INSTABILITY

Political and economic stability can help in implementing the welfare programmes. The political instability has serious repercussions on equity and social justice. The position of direct foreign investment in China and India is a pointer to this truth. China with Communistic governance and even with complaints of human rights violations from Capitalistic world has been able to attract more direct foreign investment as compared to India with a democratic system. China's foreign investment amounted to 120 billion dollars compared to India 12 billion dollars. In China, non-Chinese foreign investment is 13% as compared to India where non-Indian foreign capital is only 1% of total investment. In China, rules of game are well laid down and strictly enforced but in our case political instable environment had serious adverse effects. The instability suits certain classes who benefit from uncertainties and the damage is done to weaker sections of the society. Political instability most adversely affects the system of governance of our welfare programmes.

ACCUMULATED INEQUITIES DISPARITIES AND GROWING DIFFICULTIES

We have been expressing our commitment to equity, social justice and abolition of regional and personal inequalities but we have been witnessing the process of erosion. There seems to be no monitoring of this accentuation of inequity and disparity in the growth process. In the fiftieth year of Independence we are again reaffirming the task of building equitable society and concentrate on hitherto neglected sectors of primary education, health, employment generation and welfare of the weaker sections of the society, though the task with process of time has become formidable. To illustrate, in the field of primary education if our new commitment is to be implemented as one study shows that there will be the need for 13 lakh school rooms and 740 thousand teachers. Even if the present enrolled strength goes to school the share of space for each child will be 18 inches which is obviously inadequate. About 48000 villages do not have primary schools. The financial allocation on primary education will have to be raised to 6% from existing 3.7%. Even the regional disparities are serious. The percentage of eligible students not going to school in for northern states of Uttar Pradesh, Madhya Pradesh, Bihar and Rajasthan is 60% while in four southern states of Andhra Pradesh, Tamilnadu, Karnataka and Kerala it is 25%. In the area of public health our investment has been 1.7% against the world average of 9%. With poor preventive measures and health awareness sometimes alarming developments take place as UN reported that India has the largest HIV infested population which is growing rapidly. If reasonable progress has been made from the beginning and the enforcement and implementation of social sector and welfare programme had been maintained these problems would not have accumulated and this task would not have been in this gigantic and challenging form.

REGIONAL DISPARITIES AND CONSTITUTIONAL GUARANTEES

Regional disparities have assumed serious dimensions. In our plan documents and policy pronouncements, we laid great priority to the objective of removing regional disparities and balanced regional development. But the whole process of economic development and fiscal operations so developed that the process of inequity could not be checked but was accentuated. The relevant studies almost unanimously confirm that regional disparities have been increasing overtime. There may be regional variations in various indicators like per capita income, growth rates, human development index, poverty ratio, availability index of education, health, housing facilities but the broad conclusion is that regional disparities have been increasing. The gap between the rich and the poor states has been widening. If we see the figures of percentage share of population and percentage share in GDP (in brackets) this will give some idea. Bihar 10.21 (5.18), UP 16.44 (11.45), Madhya Pradesh 7.82 (5.48),

Rajasthan 5.20 (4.18) in all these percentage share of population is larger than that in N.N.P. The position of Bihar and Uttar Pradesh is alarming. But there are other states whose percentage share of population is smaller than that of N.N.P. Punjab 2.40 (4.06), Maharashtra 9.53 (13.18), Gujarat 4.88 (5.86), Haryana 1.95 (2.69). These are illustrative instances to demonstrate the extent of disparities. A few illustrations of per capita income differences would also illustrate the same. There are states whose per capita income is below Indian average (Rs. 5015 in 1990-91), Bihar Rs. 2539, Uttar Pradesh Rs. 3553, Madhya Pradesh Rs. 3614, Orissa Rs. 3180, Rajasthan 3983, while the other states are much above Indian average—Punjab Rs. 8281, (1) Maharastra 7409, (2) Haryana 6936, (3) Gujarat 6060, (4) The income of Bihar is half of Maharastra, Gujarat and Haryana. Some states have improved their ranking—Andhra 13 to 8, Haryana 5 to 3, Rajasthan 14 to 10 while there are states whose ranks have come down between 1960-61 and 1990-91, Assam from 7 to 15, Uttar Pradesh 12 to 13, West Bengal 3 to 6 and Tamilnadu from 6 to 9.

These facts amply demonstrate the vast disparities in income and living conditions in different states. The analysis of the disparities reveal large number of factors responsible for this. There are factors relating to natural resources and their optimum utilisation, development of infrastructure facilities, productivity, social services, health and education facilities to people, standard of governance, and political stability. These vast regional disparities and their accentuation over the last fifty years after independence raise some fundamental issues which if not raised in the past may be raised now. The constitutional prerogative is to treat all citizens with equality and justice. There should be equality of opportunity and access to basic amenities of good uniform education, health services, housing facilities, guarantee of good governance and political stability. The citizens of the country have to be treated fairly.

There is an emergent need of building a harmonious relationship between growing demand of federal decentralisation and constitutional arrangement to guarantee equal opportunities enforcement to all citizens of the country regardless of their place of domicile. If the arrangement of sharing of power and authority, command over resources, freedom to operate in own way, constitutional freedom to have autonomy of the state in allocation and distribution of resources is preparing ground for perpetuation of disparities and exploitation, the whole issue has to be examined afresh. These matters have to be examined from the point of view of the nation as a whole. There should be some constitutional amendments to ensure equality generating arrangements and disparity restraining provisions. If there are conditions in some states under which the citizens' basic human rights of equality of opportunities and availability of services of health, education, housing and sanitation cannot be protected, the nation cannot be silent spectator to their misery. If in the states there is political uncertainty, criminal domination collapse of governance, leakage and misappropriation of funds, economic stagnation, the people cannot and should not be made to suffer.

We look forward to making India of our dreams with accelerated economic development with equity and social justice and building our society free from exploitation and suffering. We have to make dedicated efforts for realisation of our objective of just social and economic order.

2

Issues and Policy Option for Health and Medical Services in India

B.M. JANI*

Growth of service sector in general and health and medical services in particular will have to play a definite and determinate role so as to improve quality of manpower for sustainable growth of a nation. The process of growth of service sector include investment in human capital through budget provisions for anti-poverty programme, literacy and education, population and family welfare, Medical and health care, development of women and children along with welfare programme of weaker section of community in India. The interim Budget of 1996-97 aims at National Health Insurance programme to cover the people living below the poverty line. It appears that the government is keen in India with strong emphasis on reduction in infant mortality rates to the levels prevailing in Kerala. There is a controversy among the economists that higher rate of growth of a nation will lead to fall in public health and medical services expenditure. Still, demand for sophisticated services will remain,

* Deptt. of Economics, Saurashtra University, Rajkot.

whereas, in the case of developing countries like India such services expenditure will rise despite the rate of growth. Transition period of such economy will lead to higher rate of population growth, largely due to rising facilities to check death rate. This does not mean that the government should not subsidise hospitals and medical expenditure.

This paper specifically addresses basic issues in social service expenditure like medical and health care with a view to know policy options in era of persistently deficit budgets both at state and centre levels. For this, the present paper is divided into three parts: the first one reviews existing literature on the subject to sort out issues, the second one reveals present scenario of funding of health and medical care expenditure both in public and private sector, whereas, the third one offers policy options to be followed by the government for sustainable growth.

I

RETROSPECT

There are several studies undertaken in India and abroad pertaining to management and financing of health and medical care expenditure in India with a view to know problems, prospects and policy guidelines. A mention may be made here to review a few of those to sort out issue.

National Institute of Health and Family Welfare (1992) carried out a study of user charges in selected localities of Delhi and come out with issue of "opportunity costs". The expenditure incurred by sample patients in the study on travel, expenses on drugs brought from market as not available in government health care was much less than the expenditure incurred for private health facilities may be given room for user charges. Health care charges in the government health system will be acceptable to the people, primarily largely due to subsidization charges levied will be lower than what is being spent in utilising private health care services. The study mentioned that time spent on obtaining health care services was higher in government facilities than private health care unit. It appears that introduction of the user fees or user charges for government run institution, people have to bear higher indirect cost for using public health care. The study revealed that compared to the non-poor, the poor are more sensible to the cost charges in health care in terms of money, quality and time spent.

World Bank study (1995)[2] explained comparative picture of health care financing for management of the budget so as to derive lessons for developing countries of Asia and Africa with international order of comparison. Techno-economic and managerial consideration play a vital role as user charges once incorporated is made by using generated additional health funds, in the case of developing countries as maintained by the study.

There are studies carried out from comparative development point of view. These include, Visaria and Gumber (1990)[3], Duggal (1992)[4], World Bank (1993)[5] so as to express disparities of available liability of health care and medical care facilities of different state level. An attempt is made to know inter-regional and intra-regional difference in India and other countries and appealed global level agencies to have new world order in favour of poorest of poor. All authors viewed that government and non-government agencies will have to work together to bridge the gap of disparities.

Studies undertaken to know managerial aspect of health care services include, Heaver (1994)[6], Gillespie and McNeil (1990)[7], Jasani and Ananthavaman (1990)[8], Pan Health Organisation (1988)[9] and Roth Gabriel (1987)[10] are drawing attention of researchers and planners all over the world. These studies have revealed interest of public and private sector management of hospital and medical facilities both in developed and the developing nations. They pleaded that non-poors fairly took advantage of government facilities and global programme of health care. Charges need to be collected on the basis of ability to pay principle for these services. All authors have mentioned arguments for privatisation of health care and medical service, for better and timely services. But conclusion generated controversy among economists and medical practitioners.

Specific studies pertaining to financing of health care,

sanitation and medical facilities are covered by World Bank (1987)[11], Khan and Prasad (1985)[12], Panikar (1979)[13], (1992)[14], Tulsidhar (1992),[15] Vogel (1992)[16], Akih and Birdstall (1987)[17], Reddy and Selvaraju (1993)[18], Seetaprabhu (1994)[19], Ravishanker (1989)[20] and others. All these studies are confined to know pattern of expenditure for health services in different states of India, alongwith financing of medical and health care services by the government and other agencies. Persistent budget deficit and balance of payment deficit created a problem to meet with rising need of health and medical care, in developing country like India. Cross-country study of World Bank also raised the issue, alongwith other issues like. Present subsidies of health services not directed towards poor, user fees in public hospital need adequate rise considering income distribution of users. Subsidies need to be targetted by differential prices of services so as to generate resources for revenue as well as appropriate use of the services. It is also argued that consumer characteristics (nature of patient and disease) should be given weightage in subsidies in medical care services. Mobilisation of resources for better hospital services created tension as demand for services is rising in relation with the supply of available services. A common argument for financing the services need financial resources from the global level of central to state level. Expenditure on instruments as well as drugs and medicine need to be increase. Classification of expenditure reveal more expenses on administration than medicine and real treatment of patients in the case of public hospitals. However, there is a gap to study expenditure pattern of public and private hospitals from financing point of view.

Issues Drawing Attention

(1) Subsidised education and health and medical services are basic indicators for higher level of living. Why is there need for re-evaluation of policy of subsidisation is desirable in the case of India?

(2) What is a basic difference in social cost and economic cost in public and private health care services in country like India?

(3) What are the alternative sources to raise revenue of

public health care services unit persistently running under heavy losses?

(4) Whether present subsidies are fully reaching to targetted poor people? What would be logic to increase user fees in the services?

(5) What kind of incentives need to be offered to non-government voluntary organisation activities of health and medical services?

(6) Why is there need to study of logic of costing and pricing of medical services considering ability to pay principle?

(7) How far privatisation of health and medical services can be considered welfare-oriented in developing country like India looking to quality of services to the users?

(8) Why entry of private sector and foreign insurance companies are welcomed in India. So, as to render health insurance services on competition basis to the users of medical and health care services?

(9) What should be the probable nature of health and medical care services sector reform in India? How they can be executed by the central and state governments?

(10) What should be strategy and policy options before government for efficient management of medical and health care services in future?

This paper is not addressing all issues but touches a few among them.

II

PRESENT SCENARIO OF FINANCING THE SERVICES

Public health and financing of public health draws attention of economists to generate infrastructure creation for essential social service like health care through medical colleges, No. of Doctors, Hospitals in the state sector. No doubt, effects of working of private sector in health which grew as much as response to the public health system. As a result of public health care, Migration of doctors from India to other developed nations decreased fair distribution of doctors for services of population. Today, State is heavily relying upon private enterprises in the provision of health care through numerous private hospitals as well as NGO sectors keeping in mind IMF, World Bank, WHO, mooted structural adjustment programme for health services have been well prepared.

After 1991 economic reforms, central and state budget for health could not brought sufficient changes as a part and parcel of reforms in health care services in India. Economic survey 1995-96 observes the allocation for health was hiked by 122% over the past three years, for family welfare, it increased from 10.6% in 1992-93 to 58.1% in 1995-96, and women and child welfare expenditure increased above 61.5% between 1992-93 and 1995-96. Looking to budget provisions and expenditure, it shows rising picture but considering actual demand for health care services, it is grossly inadequate. So, as to cope with reform in health care services. This is so as birth rate per 1000 of population came down to 28.6 in 1994 from 39.9 in 1951. Similarly, death rate has fallen to 9.2 in 1994 from 27.4 in 1951 and infant mortality rate fell down to 73 in 1994 from 146 in 1951. Still however, all rates are very high looking to figure of developed countries like Switzerland, USA, UK and other countries.

Expansion of health services reveal that number of hospitals were 2694 in 1951 increased to 13692 in 1992. Similarly, dispensaries increased from 6515 to 27403. Number of doctor increase from 61840 in 1951 to 410875 in 1992. Economists and professionals viewed that per village, per hospital per doctor service to population indicate low facilities of medical and health care in India. Central plan outlay for programmes of the development of health has been stepped up from Rs. 302 crore in 1992-93 to Rs. 670 crore in (BE) 1995-96. A substantial portion of outlay includes for allocation for the control of major communicable diseases.

The provision of health-related commodities and services offers opportunities for price discrimination as resale of the product is virtually impossible. Therefore, in Indian context price discrimination in public hospital and health care centres has not been encourage. As a result, both, rich and poor pay the same price for the service. Sometimes, rich often get subsidised services than poor. Again in marketing of health product, the consumer losses are largely due to the doctor who makes the purchase decision for the consumers.

There are variations in number of days hospitalised among the states in India. The information provided by the NSS for the year 1986-87, reveal average cost of treatment per day which is lowest in Kerala Rs. 36 for rural population compared to Rs. 91 for Haryana and Punjab. The cost of treatment was double that of Kerala, in U.P., Maharashtra and Bihar. The cost of treatment include payment made to hospital the cost of medicine, investigation and other tests. The cost is combined of rural and urban sector as well as of public and private hospitals.

It is visualised that cost of treatment is two to five times in other states than that of Kerala. The cost of treatment in government hospitals is very high relative to mark up cost in private hospital in all states of India. A rural patient in Bihar pays 6 times and one in U.P. 9 times of the amount paid by rural patient in Kerala. Table 1 provides detail of indices of hospital charges considering Kerala government as 100.

It appears from the table that medical care costs are high precisely in those states where health care facilities are widepspread. Moreover, it is possible that states having higher level of poverty indicate high cost structure owing to disease wise requirement of treatment. The cost of urban treatment in private hospital is higher in the case of West-Bengal, Maharashtra, Jammu and Kashmir relatively to government treatment in hospital. In the case of rural private hospital, Punjab, West Bengal and Haryana are states where patient pays fairly higher amount than any other states in India.

Similarly, treatment in urban government hospital is concerned Tamil Nadu and U.P. patient pay higher amount than the patient of other states in India. Whereas, in the case of rural government hospitals patients of Haryana and Himachal Pradesh pay highest amount for hospital charges. Still however, to know correct picture, it is necessary to know burden of

TABLE 1

Indices of Hospital Charges (Kerala Govt. = 100)

State	*Government*		*Private*	
	Rural	*Urban*	*Rural*	*Urban*
Andhra Pradesh	298	99	429	503
Assam	286	139	354	1394
Bihar	340	224	601	540
Gujarat	300	420	633	1044
Haryana	495	88	942	810
Himachal Pradesh	460	303	768	267
Jammu & Kashmir	326	336	728	1625
Karnataka	245	458	915	1029
Kerala	100	195	355	482
Madhya Pradesh	217	172	610	513
Maharashtra	383	349	787	1685
Orissa	194	185	446	559
Punjab	358	243	1059	1308
Rajasthan	236	307	495	428
Tamil Nadu	302	637	595	935
Uttar Pradesh	262	597	849	964
West Bengal	276	331	986	1917

Source: Morbidity and Utilisation of Medical Services, WSS 42nd Round (1986-87), *Sarvekshana*, 51st Issue, April-June 1992.

treatment charge as percentage of Net Domestic Product of different states of India. For bottom 10% of the population, the relative treatment in government hospital is below 30% in Kerala, Tamil Nadu and West Bengal with 100 to 230% burden in Assam, Bihar, Haryana, Punjab and U.P. The burden of treatment for the top 10% of the population varies between 3 and 40% in rural and between 4 and 35% in urban sectors in government hospitals.

The burden is high for treatment in private hospital but is much lower for the rich than for the lower-income groups. Therefore, the government is under impression that the public health care system provides free treatment to the poor but reality is different even upper-income group people enjoy substantial health care subsidies. A new economic policy is required to cut subsidies going to upper class. Ability to pay principle to be adopted for non-poors.

The logic for higher burden for medical treatment is obvious for several reasons. For this Table 2 indicates burden of

TABLE 2

Burden of Disease by Age and Sex in India: 1990

Age Group	*Millions of Liability Adjusted Life Years (Daily) Lost*			*% of Lost*	*Daily per 1000 Population*		
	Male	*Female*	*Total*		*Male*	*Female*	*Total*
0-4	67.3	70.0	137.2	46.9	1125	1234	1178
5-14	15.8	16.5	32.3	11.1	155	173	164
15-44	30.8	35.0	65.8	22.5	154	191	172
45-59	16.5	12.3	28.9	9.9	348	268	308
60+	14.9	13.3	28.2	9.6	500	460	480
Total	145.3	147.1	292.4	100.0	331	359	344

Source: World Development Report, 1993, p. 215.

disease by age and sex for the year 1990 in Indian case. It is evident from the table that meant mortality and disability of life is higher between 0 to 5 year of age than economically active population group of 15-44 age group. However, in the case of female, they are highly affected in both the group of age. Thus, female health care need due weightage in India in public health programmes. Similarly, Table 3 reveals burden of

TABLE 3

Burden of Disease by Consequence, Sex and Age: 1990

Age Group	*As a result of premature death*			*As a result of disability*		
	Male	*Female*	*Total*	*Male*	*Female*	*Total*
0-4	53.0	55.1	108.1	14.2	14.9	29.1
5-14	9.4	10.8	20.2	6.4	5.7	12.1
15-44	18.9	17.7	36.6	12.0	17.2	29.2
45-59	9.8	7.3	17.2	6.7	5.0	11.7
60+	9.7	8.7	18.4	5.2	4.6	9.8
Total	100.8	99.7	200.6	44.5	47.4	91.9

Source: World Development Report, 1993, p. 221.

disease and as a result premature death. The age group 0-3 years of age and 15 to 44 years of age are victim of diseases. Relative figure of female death is higher than female for the data 1990. Similarly, disability in both the age groups for female are higher than male. This has happened largely due to poor service of clinics, shortage of drugs, transportation and maintenance over and above poorly managed hospital in India in general and rural area in particular. The government pays too much for drugs of low efficiency and drugs supplies are stolen or go waste in hospitals. Policy-makers should see allocative efficiency, technical efficiency and efficient health care services reaching to poors.

III

POLICY OPTIONS TO BE FOLLOWED

(1) Health care service subsidies may be targetted through differential pricing of service in urban and rural area so as to reduce disparities of services, generation of revenue and to encourage appropriate use of the services. The new view of social sector pricing in general and health care service in particular at heavy per unit subsidy through uniform low or zero prices accompanied by quality rationing when budgets are tight. For this, price differential is welcomed through services consumed by the rich and increase subsidies for those consumed by the poor.

(2) In a developing country like India, proper data need to be generated by health department regarding user fees, revenues, services availability, income-group-wise use of such services for proper action plan for pricing and revenue of health service. Free or heavily subsidised provision of social services has not led to adequate access to the poor.

(3) There is little availability regarding cost structure of social services like health care in India. In most of the cases, Marginal cost is assumed constant but in reality it is varying. Cost function consistent with economic theory need to be estimated. This is so as fee raising involve scale, scope and availability of health services in a particular area or a hospital.

(4) Looking to failure of health services in prominent hospitals, efficient services of health care required for all class of people in India. Quality of services should be assured on one hand and on other hand failure need to be compensated in the case of gross negligency on the part of providers of health service.

(5) Government actions are required to compensate for problem generated by uncertainty and Insurance market failure in a country like India, uncertainties are pertaining to probabilities of illness, efficiency and efficacy of health care, shortcomings of operation on patients failure of cases in hospitals need health risk incentives for insurance companies. There may be moral hazard in insurance industry reduces incentives for individual to avoid risk. When the government is directly involved in health services by providing health programme or financing essential service for poor, it would be a problem for policy-makers regarding efficient allocation of resources. It is a tendency of donors to maximise health gain for the money spend by them.

(6) The Role of the government would be vital in the market of health by disseminating health-related service of control of contiguous disease. Provision of cost effective service to the poor is an effective and acceptable approach to poverty reduction in a country like India. Investment in health service by the government, NGOs, Private Sector and by Charity Trust appear to be absolutely necessary in India as, funding of health service cannot be met by government only. Massive efforts are required in order to achieve the goal of health for all.

(7) There is a need for preventive action stopping disease spreading through polluted water and non-hygienic food in developing country like India by executing proper law and order for supplies of water and food in the society. Public health programme should aim to stop disease which can substantially reduce cost of health care from family budget. Proper senitation programme in favour of poor and slum-dwellers need to be executed those who are victim of disease the first.

(8) There is a need to raise more medical colleges, number of nurses, hospital-beds in all states of India so as to increase

per doctor, per nurse or per hospital availability of medical care services for both in urban and rural area. Privatisation of medical and engineering colleges have resulted in private business to charge higher fees along with capitation fees for medical students. Supreme Court ruling failed to give clear cut idea about what constitutes capitation fees. Nor, it has directed the government to fund medical education on a large scale. Such ambiguities gave a birth to private medical college and institute which have become major industry in India. The responsibility has been shoulder to the state government to see new private such colleges to prohibit from charging more than Rs. 2000 per term fees from any student in the case of India.

(9) There is a need for a New Economics Health order under funding for health facilities by global level agencies in favour of the third world countries as local resource for health care service as grossly inadequate for mass health care programme in India.

(10) Economists have advocated for clear cut nature of health financing and health funding under financial sector reform in India. Innovation in financing medical education credit and charges in health insurance service to cope with their rising cost. There is a need for entry of foreign as well as private sector health insurance companies in India to cover weaker sections to avail all types of health care service. Thus, insurance industry require structural changes to support financial sector reform in India. In the case of environmental pollution, sanitation and related services are as essential preventive components of public health interventions, cholera, small pox, dysentery require hygienic water and proper drainage services for better health. It is a fact that curative services have controlled mortality and not morbidity which continues to rise. A focus on linkage between deprivation and ill-health also draws attention of authorities that poor health is not "Medical Problem". Merely expanding health service will not serve the purpose but also several human dimensions require due weightage for Manpower development in any country.

CONCLUSION

It is true that free or highly subsidised social service like health care service have not led to adequate access for the poor. There is missing link in research of ability and willingness to pay for health service against technical assessment of technical, administrative and economic costs for targetted health services. There is a case to accept pricing reform for high cost health service so as to raise revenue of the services and fair distribution of health subsidies. More systematic evaluation of social sector price and subsidies need due attention of planners and researchers through reliable data. Pricing policy for health services should aim, resource mobilisation, promotion of efficiency and equity too. As a part of insurance sector reform, entry of private sector and foreign insurance companies encouraged for better health care insurance service through competitive insurance market.

Notes and References

1. National Institute of Health and Family Welfare, Price of Health Care Services among Poors of Delhi, NIHFW, 1992.
2. World Bank, An Assessment of Health Care Financing: Lessons for Developing Countries, World Bank, Washington DC, 1995.
3. Visaria, Pravin Gumbar, Difference in Utilisation of Health Services in Western India (1980-81 to 1986-87), 1990.
4. Duggal Ravi, Regional Disparities in Health Care Development: A Comparative Analysis of Maharashtra and Other States, NCAER, Delhi, 1992.
5. World Bank, World Development Report: Investing in Health, Oxford University Press, 1993.
6. Heaver, G., Managing Primary Health Care: Implication for Health Transition, World Bank, Washington DC, 1995.
7. Gillespie, Stuart McNeil, Geraldine, Food Health and Survival in India and Other Developing Countries, Oxford University Press, 1990.
8. Jesani, A. Ananantharaman, S., Private Sector and Privatisation of Health Services, ICSSR, Bombay, 1990.
9. Pan Health Organisation, "Financing Health Services in Developing Countries: Agenda for Reform", Bulletin, 22, No. 4, 1998.
10. Roth, Gabviel, The Private Provision of Public Services in Developing Countries, Oxford University Press, New York, 1987.
11. World Bank, Financing Health Services in Developing Countries, A World

Bank Policy Study, Washington DC, 1987.

12. Khan, M.E. Prasad, C.V.S., Health Financing in India: A Case Study of Gujarat and Maharashtra, Operations Research Group, Baroda, 1985.
13. Panikav, P.G.K., "Resources not the Constraint on Health Improvement: A Case Study of Kerala", *Economics and Political Weekly*, Vol. 14, No. 44, 1979, pp. 1803-09.
14. *Ibid.*, "High Cost of Medical Care in Kerala: Tentative Hypothesis", *Economic and Political Weekly*, June 6, 1992.
15. Tulsidhav, V.B., State's Financing of Health Care in India: Some Recent Trends, Institute of Public Finance and Policy, New Delhi, 1992.
16. Vogal, Ronald, J., "Cost Recovery of Health Care Sector: Africa, World Bank Technical Parler, No. 82, Washington DC, 1992.
17. Akih, John, C., Birdstall, Nancy, "Financing Health Services in LDC", Finance and Development, June 1987, pp. 40, 43.
18. Reddy, K.N., Selvaraju, V., "Health Care Expenditure by Government of India: 1974-75 to 1990-91, National Institute of Public Finance and Policy, New Delhi, 1993.
19. Seeta Prabhy, K., "Financing Health Care Sector in Maharashtra", The Indian Economic Association, 76th Annual Conference Volume, 1994.
20. Ravishanker, V., India: Government Expenditure on Social Services, 1976-77 to 1986-87, World Bank, Washington DC.

3

Political Economy of Social Sector Development in India

A.D.N. Bajpai*

INTRODUCTION

The social sector, *per se*, has gathered more significance during post new-economic policy regime. The NEP-91 is founded on the principles of market economy in which major responsibility of development is rested on private sectors and remainders like social sectors are left to the state for the reason that the private sector can not take care of this sector. In the present paper an attempt has been made to define social sector and the activities, covered under this (Part I), the growing models and principles for social sector development (Part II), the progress of social sector development in India (Part III), examination of the roles of government, private and NGO's in developing social sector (Part IV) and political, social, economic compulsions of developing social sectors and indispensability of the state in its development (Part V).

* Reader and Head, Department of Post-Graduate Studies and Research in Economics, R.D. University, Jabalpur, M.P.

I

THE CONCEPT OF SOCIAL SECTOR

Albeit it is very difficult to differentiate social sectors and economic sectors from the total structure of economy because it can not be said that pure economic sectors do not have any social component and pure social sectors do not have any economic component, even then, it is generally believed that the section of population which can not help on its own or whose purchasing power does not permit to have full access to the market for their fulfilment of needs or in other words the market forces, *per se,* do not cover them are included in social sector for which special facilities like education, health, employment, etc. are to be made available without which, quite possible, their lives could have been more pitiable and miserable.

The common minimum programme of the United Front Government which was declared in June 1996 express strong commitment to the development of social sectors for achieving social justice. The commitment of the government to reflected in the enhanced central plan and non-plan allocations in the previous budget (i.e. 1996-97). The governments allocation on social sector as percentage of GDP at market price increased from 0.91% in 1992-93 to 1.19% in 1996-97. It is a positive sign in the direction of developing social sector but can it be said sufficient to meet the requirements of about sixty to seventy per cent population of India?

In the present context it will be apt to mention the major schemes covered under social sectors:

1. Education including elementary and adult education.
2. Health.
3. Family welfare.
4. Women and child development including integrated child development services.
5. Welfare.
6. Rural development including Jawahar Rozgar Yojana,

Employment Assurance Scheme, National Social Assistance Programme, IRDP, Rural Water Supply and Sanitation, Indira Awas Yojana and National Wells Scheme.

7. Other programmes like Nehru Rozgar Yojana, Scheme for Self-employment for Educated Unemployment Youth, Prime Minister's Rozgar Yojana.

The conference of Chief Ministers on Basic Minimum Services held in New Delhi on 4th and 5th July 1996 avowed the following commitments to be achieved by 2000 A.D.

1. Cent per cent coverage of provision of safe drinking water in rural and urban areas.
2. Cent per cent coverage of primary health services in rural and urban areas.
3. Universalisation of primary education.
4. Provision of public housing assistance to all shelterless poor families.
5. Extension of mid-day meal programme in primary schools to all rural blocks and urban slums and disadvantaged sections.
6. Provision of connectivity to all unconnected villages and habitates.
7. Streamlining the public distribution system targeted to below poverty line.

The above mentioned schemes and programmes are directly addressed to meet the requirements of those who do not have an access to the market forces which means they are not in a position to purchase the goods and facilities at market prices. The commitment of the government, so far as social sector is concerned, has been being reflected in all its documents but it has become more prominent in the phase of New Economic Policy.

II

GOVERNING MODELS OF SOCIAL SECTOR DEVELOPMENT

India has been progressing, although at a slow pace, from the very independence and the Nehru-Mahalanobis strategy of mixed economy has been influencing the policy-makers and the policies of the government as well with some variations on the either side. But since June 1991 the N-M model has been almost thrown out and replaced by market economy model based upon privatisation, liberalisation and globalisation in which there exists very little place for social sector. The market friendly model which is accepted by the government and started implementing in the practice also believes, that the government should act in accordance with the messages coming from the market and corporate with them. The market in turn means 'The demand forces' which are synonymous to the purchasing power. It means that the government should cooperate with the persons/agents who have sufficient purchasing power and share the responsibility of development with them. It takes us to the old classical model in which *laissez-faire* was controlling the eco-dynamics. The system, motivated by the instinct of self-interest, activated by the instrument of price, and dictated by the conditions of profit in market economy system in which private sector plays a dominant role. The private sector can very well take care of his individual interests and be a successful economic agent but it can't take care of his individual interests and be a successful economic agent but it can't take care of societal needs especially of those who are distressed, depressed, and poverty stricken. Hence, the government has to come forward to protect the interests of this section of population whether it be urban slum-dweller or rural poverty-striken, landless labour or forest villagers, etc. This is why several concepts like 'Safety-Net', 'Development with Human Face', etc. are in currency. In a nutshell, it can be said that the present model believes in the strategy in which forces of economic growth be controlled by the private sector and that of the social justice be managed by the government.

III

DEVELOPMENT OF SOCIAL SECTOR IN INDIA

It will be useful in the present context to take an account of social sector development in India to have a first hand idea of the scenario.

The per-capita income at constant price has increased from Rs. 1127 in 1950-51 to Rs. 2593 in 1995-96. The present per capita income at current prices is reported to Rs. 9321 which means about Rs. 777 per month and about Rs. 26 per day. One can very well imagine how a person can lead a respective life from Rs. 26 per day.

In real terms if a study is made about the availability of some basic items it is found that in 1951 only 334 grams of cereals per day was available which has increased to 464 grams in 1996. On the other hand, the availability of pulses has gone down from 60.7 gram per day to 34.0 gram per day during 1951-96. It means a common Indian can have only about 464 grams of cereals and 34 grams of pulses per day which can not be said sufficient by any norm. Similarly, for other commodities it is found that an average Indian consumer 7.2 kgs of edible oil in a year, 1.0 kgs of vanaspati, 14.1 kgs of sugar, 28 meters of cloth, these are bare averages. The actual consumption of downtrodden is many times less than these averages. Although the literacy rate has increased from 18.3% level to 52.2% in 1991 but still female literacy is just 39.29%. It means that still about 48% of India's population in general and about 60% of female population is illiterate. So far as drinking water and sanitation facilities are concerned, it is found that in 1985 only 56.3% of rural population and 72.9% of urban population was covered by drinking water facility which has increased to 80% and 85% respectively in 1996. Similarly, the coverage of sanitation facilities has increased from 0.7% in case of rural population to 4.64% during 1995-96 and from 28.4% in case of urban population to 50.5% during the same period.

From this it may be inferred if official data is reliable that still 18% rural population and 15% urban population of India does not have an access to safe drinking water. Moreover, about 95% of rural population and 50% urban population does not have proper sanitation facilities. Further, India has only 48 recognised medical practitioners per 10,000 of population and 9.6 hospital beds per 10,000 population which shows the utter inadequacy of medical facilities. Besides the above indicators about 48% of total population living below poverty line itself speaks about the social scenario.

IV

ROLE AND RESPONSIBILITY OF DIFFERENT AGENCIES IN SOCIAL SECTOR DEVELOPMENT

The above discussion about the present status of social sector in India reveals that the state cannot leave the fate of underprivileged class to the exploitative market force. The government of India has been allocating funds on the development of these sectors but that is not sufficient in looking into the requirement. For example, in 1996-97 budget the government allocated Rs. 3388 crore for education, Rs. 815 crore for health, Rs. 1535 crore for family welfare, Rs. 847 crore for women and child development, Rs. 940 crore for welfare programmes, Rs. 8632 crore for rural development and Rs. 220 crore for other employment programmes like NRY, PMRY, etc. The total allocation on the major scheme of social sectors accounts only 1.19% of GDP at current price.

No doubt, the government has been allocating funds for the development of social sectors but actually whether that allocation reaches to the targeted population is a matter of serious concern. Our late Prime Minister Shri Rajiv Gandhi said that only 15% to 20% of total allocation reaches to the persons for whom the programmes are made and allocation is released. It means that 85% to 80% of total resources are not being utilised for the social sector development. Here lies the paradox. On one hand it is recommended that the government should bear the responsibility of social sector because the private sector does not have the social commitment and on the other hand the government is not competent enough to monitor the fund flows and utilising it efficiently.

As an alternative to the above pure private sector and the government sector, the Non-Government Organisations (NGO's) are presented with an objective that they will act according to the instincts of social commitment and utilise the resources efficiently. But stories of NGO's are also not secret to the common man. Leaving very few NGO's in India other are just behaving like any government organisation. Their main purpose is to get good amount of resources from the government in the value of social sector development and consume them extravagantly. Needless to mention that some NGO's do not have any *locus-standi* they are created on the paper's only but due to their good linkage with the politician and bureaucrats they are getting good funds without having any effective control. Some NGO's develops international linkage and get funds from those agencies. In this connection I would like to make it very clear that while commenting upon the role and functioning of NGO's, I never mean that there are not good NGO's. There are some NGO's performing their role in the most effective manner. But these are only in exceptions and exceptions do not quantify for generalisation. Therefore again a paradox is encountered and a thinker finds win in total bewilderness. The private sector, in state sector or NGO's all are incompetent to solve the problem, and finally our attention casts around the state. The commitment which a state may have for social sector development, no other agency may have. In this respect a comment on democracy is essential.

V

POLITICAL, SOCIAL, ECONOMIC CONSIDERATIONS OF SOCIAL SECTOR DEVELOPMENT

Indian polity is committed to democracy, in which it is presumed that each citizen has equal opportunity to develop himself. Further the government is also supposed to take full care of the needs and requirements of common Indians. The government is also supposed to be secular in the sense that it will not bring any religion, caste, colour, creed, region, gender and language bias in the policies and actions. It means that the government is meant for all and not for few, for the masses and not for the class. Further democracy is run by the people, through its elected representatives which in turn fetches significance to the election. The General-elections are integral part of a democratic system. Needless to mention that each individual gathers utmost importance in elections. The 'vote' is as secular as democracy. It does not know whether it belongs to any religion, caste, creed, colour, region, language, medium and gender. The democratic government based upon 'vote-instrumentalists' will have to be secular (unbiased) because the vote is secular (unbiased). Because the 'vote' is intrinsic in a human body, human body becomes important for all political parties contesting elections. Hence the parties in the power or out of power attempt vigorously to attract the individuals to vote for them. Withstanding, the parties in power have immense opportunity to impress the vote-bank at the cost of public exchequer. The elected members who constitute the government try to infuse their ideology in the society. Come what may, any government, any party in power can not remain unassociated from the concern of common man. Rather it will pay more attention towards their welfare. Indeed the concept of 'welfare-state' has flourished in the hands of democracy. The rudiments of 'welfare-state' and social sector development are almost the same. The government has to take care of social sector on account of the fact that major chunk of voters (rather easy votes) belongs to this section only. Thus, the government has to play a significant role in social-sector developments. In other words, no government can rule the country for a long-run without sufficiently caring for the 80-90% of population (votes) which is covered by the social-sector. Needless to mention the ever-fluctuating nature of our polity and party-power nexus has been due to neglect of down-trodden, poverty-striken and those belonging to SC/ST etc. Further, mere lip-services can not work. Albeit the government, after one another has been sloganising poverty removal programmes and investing a huge amount of resources in the name of social-sector development but due to lack of commitment the sector could not be developed as desired. From this discussion it can be inferred that the social sector development is not merely a responsibility of the state but a democratic compulsion also. The state may talk of privatistion, liberalisation and globalisation, market economy, etc., but it cannot afford to neglect the social sector in a democratic setup like ours.

Besides the above if we analyse the development of social sector from purely economic point of view we find that neglect of this sector will weaken the demand as well as supply forces of economy leading to slow growth-rate in long-run. This can be further explained like this that investment in the social sector means more investment in the quality of work-force.

If the quality of work-force ameliorates by way of making proper permission of drinking water, education, health and other facilities, their efficiency is bound to increase which might reflect in the productivity. It is an estimate, that the labour productivity of Indian labour is none of the lowest in the world because the states could not properly channelised the resources towards the social sector development. In essence, additional allocation in the social sector might improve the quality of labour which in sequence may improve the productivity and output. On the other side the additional transfer of paradoxing power in the hands of those whose marginal propensity to consume is many times more than an average Indian. In such a manner, investment in social sector strengthless the demand force which acts as a stimulic for producers and entrepreneurs. Thus the social sector investment translates latent demand into effective demand which is essential for growth. In this context it can be said that during short-run it may be possible to achieve high growth rate by manipulating the value-added generation of some high yielding sector of the economy but in long-run until and unless the social sector is brought into the mainstream continuous development, a sustainable higher growth rate cannot be achieved.

Equality may be another concern for social sector development. The process of development especially in our country has accentuated income disparities. The gulf between the rich and poor has increased. Purchasing power is getting more and more concentrated in the hands of first decide of the population. No doubt, the government is taking care of reducing absolute disparities but what about the relative disparities. No matter each person gets minimum to eat, clothe and shelter himself but suppose if one section of population is prospering out of proportion, it will certainly hurt the feelings of those who are in a position to grow in the former's comparison. Hence there is a necessity to minimise the gap, may, develop a policy through which the gaps keeps on narrowing down with the pace of time and touching the level of new or insignificant disparity, for this it is essential that the state makes a heavy investment in social-sector in order to provide the unprivileged sector much higher income than the privileged one. No economy can sustain grooming disparity in the long-run. The considerations of disparities has major social implications and also the political. The economic disparities many a times gives birth to the social tension and political distance.

VI

CONCLUDING REMARKS

In brief it may be correlated that the social sector development is not merely a societal necessity but also an economic essentiality and above all a political compulsion. The government has been investing resources for the development of these sectors but the results are not noteworthy for which two reasons are identified viz.: (i) insufficiency of resources, and (ii) improper, inefficient and ineffective utilisation of resources. Though private sector's involvement in social sector development is being advocated but its commitment to the cause is doubtful. So is the case with the NGO's. Hence ball again rolls back into the courts of public sector. Moreover in the democratic setup like ours no government can afford to neglect social sector in long-run. Hence the role of state (through government) needs to be strengthened modified to some extent in the changing scenario.

4

Social Sector and Development

NARENDR PRASAD*

INTRODUCTION

There have been encouraging signs over the past few years of a growth of scholarly interest in understanding the relationship between social sector and development. The social sectors have achieved the strategic importance for achieving the basic objectives of economic growth, equity and self-reliance by increasing the investment in human capital development. The development of human resource is vital from the point of view of economic welfare. Social scientists are of the opinion that social sector plays a dominant role in economic development and education in an important component of social sector. It is the key that opens the door to life, a necessary tool for attainment of development goals and improve the quality of human being. Arthur Lewis is of the view that "differences in countries with equal natural resources is essentially due to their manpower".[1] The differences in the level of economic development of countries is largely a reflection of differences in quality of their human resources. The values, attitudes, general orientation and quality

* Professor of Economics, Magadh University, Bodh-Gaya, Bihar.

of people of a country determines its economic development. Better people is the surest way to better society.

The present paper aims at analysing the relationship between social sector (education) and development in Indian context. The paper is organised into four sections. Section one deals with concept and significance of education and development. Section two describes the investment in education in India. Section third highlights the relationship between education and development in Indian perspective and the last section provides conclusions.

I

The role of human capital in the process of economic development has opened up new horizon in the theory of economic development. Education, being an important component of human capital, plays a vital role in economic development. As the Webster's dictionary defines, "Education" derives its origin from the Latin word "Educere" meaning knowledge and ability developed. Crow and Crow explains that "the education, of course, is a dynamic force in the life of every individual influencing his physical, mental, emotional, social and ethical development".[2] Carter V. Good observes: "Education is (i) the aggregate of all process by which a person develops ability, attitude and other forms of behaviour of practical values in the society in which he lives, (ii) the process by which people are subjected to the influence of a selected and controlled environment, so that they may obtain social competence and optimum individual development".[3] So, education determines the total ways of life.

In the early history of economic development the non-economic factors hardly found a reference in discussion on development. Meier and Baldwin has written that since the mid-eighteenth century economists devoted a large proportion of their labours to the subjects of economic development, but only a small fraction of these studies include non-economic variables.[4] The following quotation illustrates, how during the mercantalian period education of the workers was considered redundant. "Reading, writing and arithmetic are very necessary to those whose business requires such qualifications but where people's livelihood has no dependence on these arts, they are very pernicious to the poor who are forced to get their daily bread by their daily labour".[5] Then onward the economic importance of education occupied a central position in classical political economy. J.R. Culloch wrote: "An ignorant and under educated people, though possessed of all the materials and powers necessary for the production of wealth are uniformly junk in poverty and barbarism".[6] Infact, Marshall gives a full and systematic consideration to the place of non-economic variables including education in economic development are recognised the limits of economic anlaysis with purely economic factors and used non-economic factors in his holistic depiction of economic development.[7] Max Weber made intensive use of socio-economic variables in his treatise. Bauer considered non-economic factors more crucial than economic factors of development are wrote "capital resources", which are often thought to be crucial are usually less important.[8] Adelman and Marris also observes that the social and economic variables play a significant role in the process of economic development.[9] Education is necessary even for the proper utilisation of technical development. Education is the instrument for bringing about social transformation and for making democracy a success. Education is an integral part, an inescapable and essential part of the development process itself. Halsey has observed that "education has become part of the economic foundation of modern society, a central agency of social distribution and consequently an object of political debate and social policy as urgent and as important as poverty, sickness and unemployment".[10]

Development is a very elusive concept. The term 'Development' suggested by dictionary is a passage from lower stage to a higher stage which means improvement. In a technical sense development refers to qualitative and structural changes in the state of an economy. Development is much more than a process of economic growth and increasing national income. In fact, it is part of a process of social change and ethical values that leads to the creation of a whole new society.

In recent years, the meaning of development has shifted

from economic improvement to improvement in human resources. Human development has been instrumental accelerating economic growth.[11] Education improves human resources. It is well granted fact that education is the most important identifiable single factor for the improvement on private return, creation of an orderly social live based on the values of social economic justice, freedom and equality of opportunities and raising the general economic condition.[12]

II

In modern society, education is closely related to several social factors from both the individual and societal points of view. In India, society education is one of the major bases of socio-economic progress of the society and individual. Burton observes "being . . . so focussed with occupations that it may be seen as a part of economic foundation of society."[13] Investment may take the form either of investment in material or in human capital. The investment in second form makes the worker himself more efficient . . . specialised knowledge and general understanding.[14] The economic performance of a country depends on certain qualitative and quantitative characteristics of its manpower and any investment on education influences such qualitative and quantitative factors to a great extent. Investment in education is a nation's wealth in its people. The expenditure on education can be viewed as social investment in man that ultimately enhances the productivity of the labour force. It is imperative to put greater emphasis of human resource investment through investment in education.[15] The economics of growth lays emphasis on social factors contributing to economic growth. Hla Mint looks into the problem of economic growth "mainly in terms of increasing the rate of investment, not only in improving physical infrastructure, but also improving what may be called the social infrastructure, mainly in the level of education, research and technical skill . . ."[16]

The following Table 1 present the plan outlay on education from 1961 to 1997 in India.

The Table 1 reflects that plan outlay on education is rising in subsequent plan periods. It was Rs. 588.7 crores in 1961-66

TABLE 1

Plan Outlay on Education: Centre, States and Union Territories

Plan Period	*Amount in (Rs. crores)*	*Percentage distribution*
Third Plan, 1961-66	588.7	6.9
Annual Plan, 1966-69	306.8	4.6
Fourth Plan, 1969-74	774.3	4.9
Fifth Plan, 1974-79	1710.3	4.3
Annual Plan, 1979-80	263.0	2.2
Sixth Plan, 1980-85	2976.6	2.7
Seventh Plan, 1985-90	7685.5	3.5
Annual Plan, 1990-91	2316.5	4.0
Annual Plan, 1991-92	2599.0	4.0
Eighth Plan, 1992-97	19599.7	4.5

Source: Five year plan documents and economic surveys.

which rose to Rs. 1710.3 crores in 1974-79 and again rose to Rs. 19599.7 crores in 1992-97. But the outlay is far below the requirements to develop the vast human resource of the country. Percentage distribution of plan outlay on education is also not upto the need of the development of education which is a powerful engine of economic stability.

The share of the government in the financing educational institutions has been very high. In 1950-51 it was about 67.99% of total income of the educational institutions which rose to 93.41% in 1989-90, whereas the share from frees and endowments and other sources of educational institutions declined sharply from 20.39% and 11.62% respectively in 1950-51 to 3.55% and 3.04% respectively in 1989-90.[17] But inspite of such huge expenditure on education our educational system is not yielding an appropriate economic return on the expenditure that is being incurred on it.

III

Though economists largely confined to measuring the

contribution of education to economic development, the contribution of education is obviously not confined to economic growth and distribution. The impact of education on the whole fabric of development, whether economic, or social or political, is very significant. Education is the principle tool of social development. It develops basic skills and ability and thereby boosts productivity. Education is an instrument of social change and cultural transmission.[18] Education provides strength and resilience to people to respond to the changing situation and enables them to cause and contribute to societal development through development of attitudes, values capabilities and development of human resource is the main function of education. Education being the care input, in developing human resources, has a multiplier effect on the utilisation of all other resources. The modern education in science and technology has given incentives to the growth of industrialisation, commercial expansion of business in the urban areas which have been marked with accelerated growth in new economic opportunities and jobs. Pield (1988), Winegarden (1979) and B.G.J. Tilak (1986) have also observed that the contribution of education is significant in reducing poverty and improving income distribution, transferring sometimes resources from higher income groups to lower income groups. It is a means of increasing production capacity. In a world based on science and technology, it is education that determines the level of prosperity, welfare and security of the people. Theodare Schultz observes that "In accounting for the benefits from education, it is not sufficient to look only at the higher earnings associated with more education. There are many social benefits too . . . one of them is associated with the deceding and interpreting of new technical and economic information pertaining to production and consumption."[19]

Education is one of the agent of socio-economic change in society in general. The work of many social scientists like Brookover, Havighurst and Nengarten, Elliott, Reiss, Silverberg, Row, Damle and many others emphasize the function of education in bringing about socio-economic change in society. Education is a basic human need in itself, it is a means of meeting other basic needs and is an activity that sustains and accelerates over all development.[20] Education is not only of direct importance to living (e.g. in broadening a person's horizon of perception and thought), it can also influence the conversion of other entitlement into human abilities (e.g., the conversion of income into nutritional capabilities). Education has strong influence on life expectancy in several countries. As the World Bank (1984) noted "the main reasons for raising life expectancy in developing countries have been better public health status, educational advances and greater political stability. Education influences demographic patterns quite significantly, influencing the choice of family size, practice of family planning methods, and at macro-levels influencing growth of total population, fertility, rates and also the very structure and composition of population. There are direct, indirect and joint effects of education on fertility. Education decreases fertility, as it has positive effects on attitude towards need for checking the population growth. Education influences the growth as well as structure of the population including its sex composition, religious and age composition.[21] R. Centres is of the opinion that education paves the way for mobility.[22] Besides, education, refines sensitiveness and perceptions that contribute to national cohesion, a scientific temper and independence of mind and spirit. Thus the evidence on the value of education in the development process is conclusive and positive.

CONCLUSION

Education in our society is considered the key that unlocks the door to modernisation, remove poverty and unemployment and reduce the population growth. Indian economy presents a paradoxical picture of extremes but there is no denying the fact that India has made considerable progress since independence in terms of increase of all types of educational institutions, volume of enrolment and the sophistication and diversification of educational programme. Inspite of such progress the monetary and non-monetary return to education trivial. It is impossible to assure a steady flow of required manpower for a modern economy unless a huge educational super-structure is build up in India. It is therefore imperative for developing countries like ours to put greater emphasis on human capital investment through investment in education. In last, it will be appropriate to quote a verse as quoted by Rathnaiah.[23]

> "By sowing seed, you will harvest once,
>
> By planting a tree, you will harvest ten-fold,
>
> By educating the people, you will harvest one hundred-fold.
>
> —*Kaun-tsu* (4th-3rd Century B.C.)

Notes and References

1. Lewis, Arthur, (1986), *The History of HRD*, George Allen and Unwin, London.
2. Crow, L.F. and Crow, A., (1955), *Introduction to Education*, Chicago.
3. Pandey, P.N., (1988), *Education and Social Mobility*, Daya Publishing House, Delhi.
4. Meier, G.M. and Baldwin, R.E., (1957), *Economic Development—Theory, History, Policy*, Asia Publishing House, London.
5. Biswas, D.K., (1979), *Society, Polity and Economy*, B.R. Publishing Corporation, New Delhi.
6. Culloch, J.R., (1943), *Principles of Political Economy.*
7. Carlier, Robert, (1975), *Non-economic factors in the Study of Economic Development*, AID, Microfiche.
8. Bauer, P.T., (1973), *Dissent on Development*, Vikas Publishing House, Delhi.
9. Adelman, Irma and Marris, Cynthia (1968), An Econometric Model of Socio-economic and Political Change in Underdeveloped Countries, *American Economic Review.*
10. Halsey, A.H., (1970), "The Sociology of Education" in Neil J. Smelse (ed.), *Sociology: An Introduction*, Wiley Eastern, New Delhi.
11. Aggarwal, B., (1988), "Neither Sustenance Nor Sustainability" in B. Agarwal (ed.), *Structures of Partsiarchy.*
12. James, M. and David, M., (1963), "Education and Income", *Quarterly Journal of Economics.*
13. Burton, R. Dark, (1962), *Educating the Expert Society*, Sanfrancisco.
14. Dalton, Hugh, *Principles of Public Finance*, 4th ed., London.
15. Prasad, Narendra, (1990), *Constraints on Rural Development*, Amar Prakashan, New Delhi.
16. Gyal D. Ness, Harper and Row (1970), *Essay in Sociology of Economic Development*, New York.
17. *Economic Survey*, 1995-96, Table 10.8.
18. Brookover, W.B., (1955), *A Sociology of Education*, New York.
19. Schultz, T., (1974), *The Education of Farm People*, Evans Brothers Limited,

London.

20. World Bank (1980), *Education Sector Policy Paper,* Washington DC.
21. Tilak J.B.G., (1992), Education, Health Nutrition and Demographic Changes—A Review of Evidence on Asia, *The Indian Journal of Labour Economics,* Vol. 35, No. 2.
22. Centres, R., (1940), Education and Occupational Mobility, *American Sociological Review.*
23. Rathnaiah, E.V., (1977), *Structural Constraints in Tribal Education,* Sterling Publications, New Delhi.

5

*Developmental Planning in the Social Sector: Indian Context**

P.C. TIWARI**

Developmental planning in the social sector is an interdependent and multisectoral process. As in all other sectors of plannings, fiscal allocations and physical targets determine the planning frame. But unlike other sectors, the quantifiable measures ends there. It is in the 'felt' perceptions, in the multiplier levels of changes and impact at individual and social levels, that seems to bear no direct relationship to the formal plan exercise that real assessment of change is possible. It becomes an area where the roles of benefactor and beneficiaries become blurred and in many cases, the beneficiaries become the benefactor, both the prime movers as well as the absorber of impact.

For want of a better identification tag both for the planners and the bureaucracy, this vague target group becomes the people. For purpose of bureaucracy—both governmental and political

* An article submitted in the 79th Annual Conference of the Indian Economic Association to be held at Jiwaji University, Gwalior, from 28-30 December, 1996.

** Reader, Deptt. of Economics, Handia Post-Graduate College, Handia, Allahabad.

'people' become a shelter for all that is done or is not done, for academicians, seminars, conferences and visibility exercises for all other types, the word 'people' becomes a mantra and a convenient tool. The 8th Five Year Plan also formalitises its homage to people. The plan document thus beings with the acknowledgements.

"Democratic planning means the harnessing of people's power and their fullest participation".

The subsequent structure of the plan does not, however, discuss either the concept of people's participation or its operational details. This omission is surprising since the plan documents has, as a system precisely defined objectives and targets. If this is not to be read as a syntactical exercise, then some basic questions needed to be answered. Who are 'People'? What form does this participation take. Is it a reference to individuals living in villages and communities? Or does it refer to organised formal political, quasi-political or other interest groups?

In the planning process in most cases, delivery systems are clearly defined. These are specifically designed schemes and projects which are to be put through existing channels of developmental administration. One broad assumption could be that the planner's perception of peoples' participation is limited to private enterprise in industrial and commercial sectors. This may mean that within the frame work of government policies and objectives, private enterprise shall have a role to play. The role of the private sector, so to speak, has in the plan context been legitimised.

The system of delivery of services in the entire range of direct social services sectors of health, education, components of Minimum Need Programme, rural development and employment programme is either controlled by the existing administrative system or a sub-system created and controlled by it. This is not surprising. Planners have viewed the social services sectors also with the same archetypical perception with which they have seen individual and commercial sectors which have well-defined and highly structured and controlled system. This culture and trend of thinking has determined the strategy in social services sectors also resulting in well defined inputs of management techniques.

In the plan document or indeed elsewhere in the governmental system, there has not been a serious experiment or even a debate at any level, about what "People's participation" means—what role it can and should have, how it can be organised and its growth sustained. Some how the basic assumptions in the plan whether in talking of employment targets, immunisation or mother and child-care has been that fiscal allocation pre-supposes the trickledown effects of the benefit. The input-output ratio approach has been extended to the social service sector also.

PATERNALISTIC APPROACH

The approach, however, is again paternalistic:

"For effective implementation of social welfare programme, local communities would be fully involved and stimulated for sharing greater responsibility in organisation and supervision. `Their participation will also be essential for identifying the beneficiaries. A system of participative decision-making by all beneficiaries at the delivery point may be considered.

In considering the delivery system in the developmental process administrative process is often taken to be synonymous with management system. It has become a cliche to say that while the plans are well-conceived, implementation is poor. Existing delivery system of developmental plans are a part of the administrative and bureaucratic process. It is not realised that the formal system is not equipped to have grassroot feel of sensitivities at first hand. A basic argument of this article is that the formal bureaucratic system cannot be changed.

Translated into operational details, planning exercises take the shape of projects which then develop their own systems are sometimes, involved in specific and limited areas. These then create their own sub-systems and bureaucracies and more or less subsist on and justify the main system—defining and enlarging it further in the process.

Inevitably, this brings up the question of concept and role of the bureaucrats *vis-a-vis* the citizens in sectors of slow growth and changes such as in the social sectors. Inputs of time, resources and costs put into this sector glaringly contrast with achievements. It may be argued that ultimately, the government is the most organised and visible and acceptable form of social structure that spends people's money and acts on their behalf. Why then should governmental system be replaced by any other form of people's action?

It need not be, if two basic assumption's are made. First, that 'government' is not synonymous with 'bureaucracy', and the second that democratic and responsible decentralisation can take place both within the system as also outside it.

FORMS OF COLLECTIVE ACTION

In the social systems today, two forms of people's collective action are available Panchayats, Zila Parishads and other village bodies have become and are fast becoming, both politicised and bureaucratised. The other is the system of voluntary groups—both with the formal legal sanction and without it 'there are' as per Central Social Welfare Board, about 12,000 such registered organisations. There are many more which function informally but no less effectively. These organisations have developed their own systems and cultures. Bureaucracy has also rubbed a part of itself on to these organisations through grant-in-aid patronages and other subtle means.

To say that a formal voluntary sector is the answer would however, be a facile generalisation.

Most voluntary agencies today are urban. A few are promoted as exercise invisibility for unsuccessful politician, idle-rich wives and similar other classes. These are basically pressure groups. They tend to take upon themselves the role of 'elites'—spokesman for all the rest. The biggest damage that these groups pose is that they become, due to their high visibility, the only perception for the policy-makers or the bureaucrats, blocking and other and creating a chasm between other agencies and between reality and policy framing.

Too often these big organisations develop their own bureaucracies—as rigid and tyrannical as any other. If then becomes a power game and in the process, it does not let any other voluntary effort grow unless it is patronised by them. It assumes an overpowering elitism and it becomes a broker, a middleman, between the people and the system. Thus it destroys more than it creates for it corrupts the system at its very source.

Bureaucracy has to react to the big 'voluntary' groups due to its own compulsions. There is the democratic compulsion, mainly as a part of parliamentary process, to promote the growth of voluntary effort. There is administrative pressure to spend the fiscal allocations. It becomes a mutually supportive partnership which promotes the grant-in-aid culture.

At other levels, the best of small agencies are alienated and good causes are killed as happens everyday in women's organisation taking up various causes through bemused apathy of an unresponsive power structure. Smaller agencies have, in any case, neither the resources nor the time to be seen or heard in the corridors of the secretariats.

Would the solution then seem to be in a kind of a midway house compromise, that does not remove the soft options but which recognises the strength of different systems.

SOCIAL AND HUMAN PERCEPTION

A basic strength of peoples' organisation is that it can respect and formalise those social and human perception that other formal system can either not systemise or can at best only reduce to a training manual. These community systems can operate on both the levels; they can use, understand and hopefully, influence governmental sub-systems. Successful voluntary efforts underscore these points, that development has a human dimension, that attitudinal elitism only brings reaction and not progress that developmental frame has to adopt itself to the socio-cultural systems and not *vice-versa*, that communication means understanding by the community and not by the media elites and finally that people—village people—are neither ignorant nor fools.

Yet in our planning process, we have institutionalised perception based on cliches. In the community health workers scheme—now the village guide schemes—the health worker is a person selected by the Primary Health Centres through the Panchayats. The scheme has not had the desired effect because most of the men selected (now health guides are women) have no involvement and the community is different. She has become an extension of the bureaucracy and is, therefore, equally suspect. However when in similar rural health projects a health volunteer has been selected through a democratic process by the villagers, he or she has succeeded. The basic point is that she had the initial approval of men in the village. In a male-dominated set up, it is the biggest social approval. Yet in trying to successfully change a project into a programme, these crucial perceptions were lost.

SOCIAL SECTOR AND OPTIMUM RESULTS

Both the bureaucratic and the voluntary systems must be then about their areas of optimum results. The governmental system has, of necessity to make resource and fiscal allocation. Since it is accountable, it has to fix broad physical targets. The community then should decide upon appropriate techniques and technologies, attitudes of systems. They can reach out to areas where little exists and fill in the gaps of planning and effort.

In a broader social sense, community groups can recognise castes and social fixities and exploit these in growth strategies. These can act as pressure groups not only within the community, but even at the level of District, State and Central Power structures. A multi-policy of such pressure groups would help in clearing planning perception and bringing some attention to low priority social sectors. At the community level, the demonstration effort of 'something done' would be a far greater catalyst of change than any big project planning.

By and large, the formal system should be willing to decentralise and delegate more, not as compulsion of a political system but with a deliberate willingness to let people decide for themselves, which means that development should be seen beyond the framework of a scheme. The bureaucratic system can, initially through a dialogue with the community, lay down broad objectives and fiscal allocations. It can monitor, evaluate the control, the allocations and the results, in partnership with the agencies. But it must not manage, nor should its schemes be as highly structured as they are. Details of work within this broad frame should be left to the voluntary agencies. It should be left free to change and improvise within this delegation. The political and bureaucratic compulsion of quickly translating a project into a programme would, to some context, be met by sacrificing finer points.

Growth of voluntary efforts should be encouraged as a part of the planning process not through a middle bureaucracy of CSWB or its State Boards or through patronage of grants-in-aids, but at a legitimate and integral part of the system. Schemes and projects should be so framed that the community can run it themselves. Involved local people should be encouraged to start such community action. More established agencies should take the role of guiding and developing these efforts. Growth of organised social efforts should be built into the district itself-not as monolithic cooperatives or such structures, but as small village-based units. In numerous women's organisations across, the country—'Mahila Mandals' and 'Mahila Sangrams'—such groups exist. There is no reason why similar groups cannot come up in other areas also. These would be local groups involved in reacting to local problems involved in reaching to local problems and accountable to the local people. District administration should help them by entrusting specific projects to these groups and build these supports in the regular fiscal and district plan. Only difference would be that instead of district administration or a big voluntary agency very many such smaller groups would be involved.

It presupposes two things, Professional voluntary work should offer the chance of a decent living to a young professional. More often initial intense involvement of a young person brings intense disillusionment when he discovers petty village politics and power games and the neglect and hostility of the people be wants to serve. It takes time to discover that people are the same everywhere and that there is no virtue in poverty. Very few, naturally, survive. If a young person is given some support, at this stage, many young people would opt for it as a vocation. Second would to be avoid the temptation to see any project as a programme and try to replicate it on a scale beyond all 'feel'. Only the growth of many such local initiatives could make it a part of the developmental processes resisting any attempt to structure it, but changing and adopting even as people, their social and other norms do changes.

References

Economic Survey's, Government of India, Various issues.

Latest Socio-economic Survey—Central-State Social Welfare Board, New Delhi, 1995.

Rajani Kothari, "Under Globalisation will Nation State Hold", *Economic and Political Weekly*, Volume 36, No. 26, July 1995.

Economy of India as reported in the ESCAP, 1996.

Socio-economic Development—An Indian Context, Dr. B.K. Tripathi.

Young Economist—Social Sector and Economic Development in India, P.C. Tiwari, Vol. 30, Aug. 95, p. 46.

6

Bonded Labour: An Analytical Study

V.P. Tripathi* and Diwakar Khare**

Inspite of the fact that India became independent more than 50 years ago and it has enacted new social legislations to check the practice of bonded labour. It is found that this nefarious and inhuman practice is still prevalent in different parts of our country. It exists in different forms in different states ruled by different political parties.

In most of the cases it is a type of labour relation between the employer and the bonded labour wherein the labour is neither free nor voluntary. The bonded person is not allowed to render labour either for his personal needs or to others in the village. The labourer is also not allowed to change his employer.

According to the Bonded Labour System (Abolition) Act, 1976 of the Government, the definition of the 'Bonded Labour System' means the system of forced, or partly forced, labour under which a debtor enters, or has, or is presumed to have entered, into an agreement with the creditor.

* Reader, Deptt. of Economics, RBS College, Agra.
** Reader, Deptt. of Statistics, Institute of Social Sciences, Dr. Bhimrao Ambedkar University, Agra.

The bonded labour system in vouge in many parts of India is a weak and distorted link in the socio-economic fabric of Indian society. It checks rural development and rural progress. It is illegal. Still several thousand young men and women are in the ring of bonded labour force.

The bonded person seldom agitates against the inhuman conditions just because both the parties have entered a sort of contract with a willing consent. The rich rules over the poor. The borrower is the Slave of the lender. In Rousseau's words, 'man is born free but everywhere he is in chains'. So is the bonded labour.

The per day remuneration of a bonded labour is extremely low and a significant part of it accounts for the value of food and clothing. Most of the bonded persons keep on working day in and day out in assurance of two square meals. On this basis it can be said that the bonded system is mainly based on pledging services in exchange of food and clothing. The labour hardly gets a subsistence minimum. The child and woman labour get less than the adult male labour.

It is an irony of fate that such a labour relation is considered a healthy mutual help agreement but actually it is not so. More bonded labour come from large poor families, generally, having more females than males. And they believe that might is right and survival of the fittest is the order of life. They are fatalists. As such mere maintenance of law and order cannot ensure liberty to human beings.

Majority of the employers of bonded labour are landlords having large holdings. They have complete faith in human enslavement or human bondage. This has been found in existence since times immemorial. Bihar is the best example to prove this.

Bonded labourers are called by different names in different parts of India such as 'Bhatua' in West Bengal, 'Baramasia' in Orissa. Bhatua is system of pledging services for a specified period, normally a year, in exchange of food and clothing plus a nominal wage.

HISTORY OF BONDED LABOUR

Servitude was quite important during the Vedic Period. They were called slaves or 'dasas', 'Shudra' or outcastes. The 'Kshatriya' clans always had 'dasas'. The 'dasa' labour was employed in agriculture and in new virgin conquered lands. Even among 'dvija' castes people become 'dasa' in return for subsistence or in default of debt. Increased debt bondage indicate increasing monetization of the economy. The modern forms of debt bondage are an outcome of this.

The Mughals employed eunuchs for guarding 'Royal Harems'. This was a barbaric institution based on human bondage. Only a small fraction of eunuchs were natural hermaphrodites. The majority were slaves cruelly mutilated in childhood.

The harsh and rigorous system of tax collection by the Muslim rulers led to pressure on the poor peasantry and to increase in indebtedness. Indebtedness and need for subsistence forced the poor to become slaves and these were treated as revenue commodity.

Under the British colonial rule the caste-linked agrestic servitude continued such as chattel slavery in the South and attachment to proprietary families. Even debt bondage became hereditary. Frequent famines and other natural disasters swelled the number of bonded labour force during the colonial rule. The British introduced the indentured labour system of recruitment of labour to other countries of British Empire. These went to South Africa, Mauritius and West Indies.

INCIDENCE OF BONDAGE

According to a joint study made by Gandhi Peace Foundation and National Labour Institute, there are 26.17 lakhs of agricultural bonded labourers in the 10 selected states of its investigation, as reported in 1981. However, at present, the number of bonded labour in the entire country is more than 30 lakhs. The largest bonded persons are in UP and MP, each having more than 5 lakhs. The other states, having more than 3 lakhs each, are Orissa and Andhra Pradesh. Tamil Nadu has

2.5 lakhs, and there are more than one lakh bonded labour in Bihar, Gujarat, Karnataka and Maharashtra. No state seems to be completely free of human bondage.

SALIENT FEATURES

1. A Form of Unfree Labour

A bonded labour often forfeits the freedom of employment or the right to move freely or the right to appropriate or sell at the market value any of his property or products of his labour.

2. Perceptual Indebtedness

The bonded labour are in perpetual debt. Indebtedness is an effective tool in the hands of Capital to enforce a control over bonded labour. In our country more than 98 per cent of the bonded labourers can be considered as in debt bondage, debt being the principal cause of their bondage.

3. Lower Castes

On account of social and cultural restrictions on the freedom of the labourers of certain castes and class, the people of this category were treated as serfs and they served as bonded labour. By and large, they belonged to the low castes having very low social status in the society. Though, mostly the bonded labour belong to lower castes but work for the high caste rich land-owing gentry. However, no high caste person would like to be bonded to a low caste employer but high caste employers always prefer to have high caste bonded labour.

4. In Human Conditions

The bonded labour are socially oppressed. They suffer from starvation, sexual exploitation, superstition, suppression of consciousness, torturous punishment, abuse, assault, frustration, intoxication and malnutrition.

5. Meagre Wages

The wages paid to the bonded labour, either in cash or in kind or in both are much below the prescribed minimum wage of the government. It is just subsistent minimum of wages. It is only a via media of assured employment compared to free labour.

CAUSES OF BONDAGE

Only those persons are forced to become bonded labour who do not have any alternative employment. They are just on the verge of starvation and in the absence of any means of livelihood, they are forced by pecuniary difficulties to go and join bondage because in this case, they at least are sure of getting two square meals per day. Thus, the root-cause of bondage is the deficit economy of the bonded labour.

Majority of the bonded labour is illiterate and, therefore, they are not aware of social welfare legislations. They have no knowledge of the "Bonded Labour System (Abolition) Act", 1976.

Another important reason for bondage is indebtedness. The poor borrow loans from the rich employers for food and social consumption, for marriage or death ceremonies, for illness or to pay past debts or government dues. The bonded persons pay back the debts in kind in the form of labour instead of cash because they do not have it.

From the employers' view point, he engaged bonded labour for his on-farm activities but he uses them for off-farm activities also such as domestic work or for grazing of cattle, etc. The employers also prefer bonded labour force because it enhance the status of the employer. At times, it may not be very profitable to keep bonded labour, still the landlords engage them as 'status' expenditure and not an inevitable and proficiable expenditure.

ATTEMPTS TO ABOLISH

In India several attempts were made to abolish bonded slavery since 1830. It started because of the progress made by the anti-slavery agitations in Britain. Legally it was abolished in 1843. But the traditional forms of servitude changed into debt bondage. The paupers and destitutes took loan and mortgaged their labour as well as that of their descendants. It is reported by *Tanika Sarkar* (1985) that the agrestic labourers in servitude made up at most 12 to 15 per cent of the work force in the 1870s and 1880s. By 1930s their relative number had more than doubled.

In the independent India, the Bonded Labour System (Abolition) Act of 1976 is a landmark legislation. It has reduced bondage but it has not been able to emancipate completely the bonded labourers. It's influence has been very limited in the absence of an alteration in the structural causes of bondage.

SOLUTION

In view of the above causes and facts, mere implementation of welfare legislation, in general, may not be the cure or solution of bondage. On many occasions, it has been observed that the net effect of welfare legislations has become negative to the beneficiaries. To cite an example, in Jaunsar Bawar of U.P., in spite of progressive government policies to free people from bondage, it has been found out that it led to the intensification of debt bondage and the introduction of prostitution for the women of the beneficiaries (Jyoti Gupta, 1985; Himalayan Polyandry: Bondage Among Women in Jaunsar Bawar).

Mere release of the bonded persons is not necessary. The eradication or rehabilitation programmes must see that the economic rehabilitation and value orientation is properly attempted and ensured. Otherwise, even a good-intentioned welfare legislation may prove futile and abortive and it may potentially intensify the bondage and suffering of the poor.

There is an urgent need to change the attitudes of the people, i.e., employers as well as employees. People must realise that 'he who oppresses a poor man insults his maker' (The Holy Bible, Proverbs, Ch. 14:31). Such a change in the mental make-up might eradicate bondage from its roots. Hence, there is also a need for psycho-social solution, in addition to, economic rehabilitation programme.

The only good sign is that the bonded labour system is decreasing with the increase in the economic status of employee household and better enlightenment of employers. The solution lies, ultimately, in a multi-pronged attack on this social as well as economic evil prevalent since ancient period.

7

Women Literacy in Rural Social Sector in India

T.K. JHA*

INTRODUCTION

Education is an essential condition for economic development. Literacy is the first ladder of it. Education is the basis of human capital development. Education develops skillness, knowledge, efficiency and abilities. For the development of the country, there is a need for the development of human resources. Human resources development is accelerated through education. The development of education in India is limited due to several historical, social and economic reasons. Consequently about half of the population of the country is illiterate. The moto of education is not only to develop man but also it is powerful means of development of social change. Literacy helps in the economic and social progress of the country. It is possible only when women should be educated alike men. The development of women is considered the symbol of development. The Indian women are the backbone of the family who help it in cooking, in upbringing children, looking

* Reader in Economics, L.N.M. University, Darbhanga.

after the members of the family. Besides it, they also do many jobs of the family. Education is indispensable for doing such kind of works.

In lack of women education, the society can not go ahead. It is the mother who imparts the basic education to her children in the family. So it is essential for mother to be educated. To educate one woman means to educate the whole family. Only an educated woman can fulfil the all round development of her children. She might lay the strong foundation of her offspring. Therefore, the education of woman means to educate the coming generation of our country.

The liberty, progress and equality of women are helpful for all round development of any nation. Male member can not eradicate poverty, unemployment, inequality and explosive population without the full co-operation of women. In fact, woman power is wonderful power of any nation whose mentality and skillness bring a new stream of life, they are utilised and used in true sense. If it goes in such way then she can provide new energy and new direction. This helps in peaceful development of nation from the point of view of religion woman has very important place in society. We can quote a saying in context of woman power—"Where woman are worshipped God resides there only". (यत्र नार्यस्तु पूज्यन्ते रमन्ते तत्र देवता:)

PROBLEMS OF WOMEN EDUCATION AND THEIR ERADICATION

In medieval India the pardah system was at climax and no attention was paid on women education. Consequently, the social and academic status of women were low and system such as, pardah system, sati-system, widow marriage system, no right of women on property mainly dominated the scheme.

In modern times some social reformers tried their level best to get the wretched condition reformed. They also laid much emphasis on their proper education. The renowned social reformers Raja Ram Mohan Roy and Ishwarchandra Bidyasagar did recommendable job for women's education. In the first phase of 19th century these reformers started a campaign of mass awakening in Bengal and efforts were taken to impart education to girls by private or social institutions. In primary school as an Inspector Vidyasagar conducted thirty-five girl schools in which he himself aided economic help to most of them. In 1949 'Bethun School', was founded in Calcutta which was the result of steps taken for women education. It was started in the fourth and fifth decade. At that it also became subject of bitter protest because some people thought that western education might be hindrance on the way of doing household and family responsibilities.

During the British reign the fundamental policy of education was to do job in offices as clerks or assistants. The government was not in touch with the spread of women education due to which women education was a little. After independence, the economical, social and cultural development were decided on the basis of planning in which emphasis was laid upon the education. As a result, remarkable progress was obtained in the field of women education. Still the ratio of women education is less than men education. For this, the social, economical and cultural factors are responsible. They have caused obstructions for their due development. Women are treated secondly in society due to which the son and the daughter are not educated alike. Most of the Indian families living in rural areas do not pay attention to girls education. They do not take it as compulsory. Whereas there is no such case in boys.

THE CONDITION OF WOMEN EDUCATION IN RURAL ECONOMY

Poverty is no less obstructive or stagnative in spread of women education. The poor classed people toil from round the clock to earn their two square of meals anyhow and are helpless to engage their offsprings in that work in order to get more wages. In this way the boy and girl who should go to school are engaged in different economic and household work and they even do not think of going to school. Most of the girls being to share their mother's work from very childhood. As a result, they even fail to see school. In this context, it is essential to say that illiteracy and ignorance of mother are of great concern as she does not think of education at all. Thus illiteracy encourages illiteracy. Such poor classed people do not have patience to send their wards to school or college keeping up the future result not to pay more attention to daily wages.

In our country most of the states take no fees in middle schools. Still most of boys and girls who take their admission, leave it after some days only. The observation shows that 75% girls leave school only after five classes. Whereas 50% girls leave their education after high school.

The main reason for this is that the high schools and colleges are very far from abode. Consequently most girls are deprived of getting higher education. For this, they need to go far of places. Their guardians do not allow them to do so. The government administration of some states of country also fail to make guardians assure to send their daughters to get higher education. The guardians feel insecurity for their daughter's return. This is also one of the reasons for which they are unable to send their daughters.

According to data of Indian census the percentage of literacy of women was only 0.6% in 1901 whereas it was 2.83% of men. In the year 1911, 1921, 1993, the percentage of women literacy was 1.05, 1.81 and 2.93.

GOVERNMENT'S EFFORTS FOR ERADICATING ILLITERACY OF WOMEN

In the beginning of present century the women movement began to be in organisational form which strengthened the women education. Mahatma Gandhi propagated much for women education and did remarkable job for their liberty. He got them joined in great number in freedom movement. The women education got special power through their awakening and co-operation. The Indian government got its constitution enforced after independence. This constitution provided equal rights to men and women in all social, economical sphere of life. The Indian government has shown a keen interest in upliftment of women, down-trodden and backward classes. Special steps have been taken for women education in social and economical development of country to keep up their contribution. The government has done praisable work time and again. The women education has got a new direction and speech after independence. In 1951 only 7.93% women of country were literate whereas after one century in 1961 this percentage increased upto 13%. According to census 1981—24.82% women of India are literate whereas this percentage for man is 46.89%. According to data of 1991 census, the percentage of literacy of country is 52.11% in which the men's percentage is 63.9% and 39.4% of women. But different states percentage is different. The lowest one is in Bihar. Here the percentage is 38.54%. The percentage of Kerala is 90.50% and Mizoram—81.23%, and Lakshadweep is 79.23%. The lowest one is of Dadar and Nagar Haveli 39.45%. In the year 1993, the literacy rate in Nepal was 74%, in Pakistan and Bangladesh 65%, in Bhutan 62% in India 52% and in Sri Lanka 12%.

We have gained only partial benefit by the new education policy enforced by the government in the year 1966-68 and 1988. Due to reckless of political and administrative arrangement. We could not get full advantage. India has got the third place for the greatest educational system. Consequently, Navodaya Bidyalay has been included in new education policy. This time there are about 206 Navodaya Vidyalas which are in practice. About one-third of them have been ensured for girls' admission. Adult education has been launched for women by social welfare board. In this form 18 to 30 years old women will be engaged for education.

EFFORTS FOR THE ERADICATION OF WOMEN LITERACY IN RURAL AREAS

According to census of 1991 the total population of women of the country is 40 crore 71 lakhs. The number of rural women is 30.5 crore. It is clear that about 81% rural women are engaged in cultivation work. It is obvious that due to poverty all poor sectioned labourers have gone to other states for their livelihood. Consequently, the cultivational work in rural areas is only done by women labourers contribution. If they do not contribute their help in cultivation due to poverty, then all cultivational work of country will be mismanaged. These 81% women population do not give their full cooperation properly to cultivational work due to illiteracy. After all whatever help is obtained in cultivational work, it is credit to them. As a result their daughters also do not go to school and they devote their time in household work. In this way the illiteracy of women is growing in country. The main remedy for the illiteracy is to educate the women upto the age of 25 to 45 through adult education. Unless they are given education, all welfare schemes would be of no use. For this there is need of regular discussion, meeting and debate so that they might be introduced to development work. They can have social understanding alongwith bookish knowledge. It needs revolution of thought. It is also need to establish a meeting place in conservation of women supervisors in villages areas where they should be encouraged to exchange of thoughts through the cultural programmes, video and television. It is certain if mothers of young girls are thoughtful and educated then they can send their daughters to school. It is evident, the girls are not sent to school due to poverty. Therefore, they must be provided all resources of education, such as slate, pencil, books, food and clothes. The former Prime Minister has proclaimed mid-day meal for children on August 15, 1995. We shall have to encourage the rural women so that they might send their daughters to school to know the distant result. They should not engage them in household works. Only educated men can increase education. So it is our foremost duty to educate the parents of women.

The policy of launching women education should be enough widespread, generous and progressive. We need such educational development from economical point of view which might be helpful in increasing productivity alongwith production. There is a need of implementation of development of women education which may reach the benefit to the weaker sectioned people alongwith production, ability to productivity and the rate of development. The reservation is not needed before brilliancy and geniusnees which instigates the class difference. Such a poor classed people who are unable to go to school due to utter poverty. The girls who are not sent to school due to illiteracy of their parents, there should be taken proper steps to overcome these things.

The Indian government lays emphasis on total abolishment of casteism on the one hand, on the other hand, encourages division of caste by granting reservation. On primary school level food should be served along with exercise book, and should make it essential for girls to go to the school. In the beginning they should be educated through their mother-tongue. In rural sector there should be free education. It should be aimed for all poor sectioned people not to mention the names of schedule caste and schedule tribes and backward caste.

The main reason of our pitiable failure on the way of reformation and eradication of illiteracy is lack of political will. It has been the great bondage on this way because the Central government has turned its face from the responsibility of educating the general people. It has given this right to state government which has not made enough efforts to fulfil this.

If we have a glance at planning of education we find in India a little part of total budget is fixed for education in comparison of other developed and developing countries. In the year 1990-91 the expenditure on total budget on education:

America	19.9%
Japan	19.6%
England	13.9%
Myanmar	11.2%
Sri Lanka	7.4%
India	1.9%

If we do not want to be trapped in any fierce or horrible distress, then first of all we will have to make our economy strong for education because the result of education comes before us after 15-20 years. The mistake that we committed 20 years ago is before us as a danger in the field of education.

After independence there were 1,72,661 primary schools, 12,843 middle schools, 5,247 high schools, 636 degree colleges, 17 universities, 17 agricultural colleges, 15 Medical colleges the number doubled in the year of 1988—We had—5,43,677 primary schools, 1,41,014 middle schools, 71,305 high schools, 9,348 degree colleges, 176 universities in which there are 17 agricultural universities and 117 medical colleges. In the whole country the proposal of 10+2+3 has been accepted in order to impart equal education to all which is the most important step.

The Indian government has taken several efforts for woman literacy and their educational development. Law has been passed from time to time. Special arrangements for women development have been taken to get fundamental or basic change in condition of women, to use education in the form of instrument, according to new education policy. The priority of starting primary schools and adult education centre has been given in rural and scheduled caste regions. The voluntary institutions have also been encouraged to launch literacy centre for women. At the advice of educational advisory council, the Indian government has got a high level committee setup for women education, which will be answerable to the progress and development of women education with the rapid growth of population of country.

The former Prime Minister, Narasimha Rao proclaimed to launch programme to provide mid-day meal in primary schools in the whole country on August, 1995 which is enforced from the 2nd October, 1995. The number of students will increase by this scheme. In some states, there is continuous increase in the presence of about 80% children in schools.

The development in modern awakening is only possible by women education. The women education should be made chief basis to take any society or on the path of development. The uneducated man construct the backward society and the backward society is great obstruction in all round development of nation.

In this way education is a national responsibility which needs the co-operation of all organisations of society in order to fulfil it. Besides the effort of government schemes, various voluntary institutions and organisations are needed to cooperate for successful abolishment in the illiteracy of women. Then only it is possible to safeguard the development of women's personality and their rights. The educated and vigil women can help in the welfare schemes and economic development of country rapidly. The efforts of government are increasing. For gaining higher education the proper educational institutions are needed so that the remote village girls may obtain higher education on the level of the rural education. In this way as a result of such efforts where in 1950-51 there were 30 universities, 700 colleges and the registered number of students was 2,63,000. Now they increased in 1993-94. The number of universities became 197, the number of colleges became 8,210 and the number of students became 50,07,000. Thus we can say that the government has taken sincere step in this direction. But the condition of education in Bihar is pitiable where the teachers working in colleges are given only 70% of their total salary. Instead of 148% D.A. only 71% D.A. are obtained. Students are not given any scholarship for many years. There is no fund for chalk and dusters consequently, the rate of literacy is the lowest in Bihar. The Chief Minister of Bihar has laid the foundation of the Charwaha Vidyalaya which is also closed in lack of finance. The money which has been invested in such schools could not be used properly.

In this way once Maulana Azad had admitted that it is essential to make the condition of teachers better and respectful. The scant salary and social prestige are reasons for such harassment on account of which there is deterioration in the qualification of teachers. That is why he considered it most essential to raise the economic condition and social prestige of teachers. He gave much importance to them after defence, grain and cloth in National Budget. Any way it is necessary to give financial aid to such programmes. As it is clear from aforesaid matters that the budget of the education in our country is less than other country of the world. It is only 1.2 per cent in our country. If we want progress in education and in women education then we will have to make it increase upto 15% of the total budget.

The primary education is needed first for progress of education in country for which the government is effortful. The Indian primary educational system is one of the largest systems of the world. Under this, there is a primary school at a distance of 1 kilometer in 8.2 lakh localities. The 94% people of country are benefited by this. In the year 1950-51 the number of high primary school was 2.23 lakhs which increasingly became 7.28 lakhs in 1993-94. There is remarkable growth in the number of school students. In 1950-51 its percentage was 12% where in 1993-94 the level of high primary education became 67.7%.

On the primary school level the number of school going girls was 52 lakhs in the year 1950-51. While this number increased and became 4 crore sixty-four lakhs in 1993-94. On high primary educational level this number became one crore 57 lakh from 5 lakhs.

If any society has to be guided on the path of progress or in the race of social, economical and political, it is possible only through education. The women education is not possible without full education, because uneducated society constructs or makes backward society and the backward society proves to be a great hindrance on the way of all round development of country.

Of course both the government and society have taken sincere effort for women education. But we can get the full women education only then when the political and administrative bodies of our country give full cooperation.

On the whole, education is essential for the development of women capital necessary for rapid economic development. The recent efforts for expanding women education, particularly in the rural area needs re-orientation and higher speed.

Human capital is one of the most crucial instrument of development and women education plays the most important role in developing human capital at every stage of development. Education supplies the economy with human resources, with requisite knowledge training and qualification to meet the demand of economic development. But we are fail to make good skilled human capital in family, society and country. Moral habits are being lost by us. At the present time we need transformation for good human capital. We have to make mode and it is only possible by education of women.

Today change is only possible by women education. When our country society and family are passing through a critical situation. The women have been holding a great importance from very beginning. Even the god Brahama (ब्रह्मा) creator, had to bent down before women and Lord Krishna feared his mother. They possess such face who can mould the spoilt family and make or mar the well-to-do family. Today it is wish of every mother to have daughter-in-law like Sita and daughter like Savitri. But this dream of mother remains merely a dream. The children have imitating nature. They do as they see. They bring up in the same way as the environment of society and family provides them.

Now-a-days real identity of women has changed. She will have to display her true character as mother and wife. When father comes back house intoxicated in midnight, he has romantic look towards his wife whom he thinks of making her beauty queen. In such circumstances, it is not easy for their offsprings to be affected by observing such drunkard situation. They even are strayed and lose their proper civility. They can not be brought on the path of civility. In this context Goswami Tulsidas (गोस्वामी तुलसीदास) has rightly quoted only women are capable for showing right direction in Kaliyug Era. (कलियुग)

It is regretable, women of today have forgotten Indian curtesy. They are indulged in some sorts of pompousness. Their running towards western civilisation is on. The women who has played a pivotal role in making man's shape changed, has lost her way. A good lady can make her daughter competent to teach her good manners and curtesy. Today people distinguish between daughter and daughter-in-law whereas daughter becomes daughter-in-law in someone's house. The incidents of activities burnt or oppressed are being printed in daily newspapers. We need to bring change in our thoughts and look. If women are determined, they can bring great change. They have played pivotal role in getting alcohol drinking stopped in many places in the country. They have got success in such struggle of course. They have great responsibility for such change. They will have to take creative step for country, society and family. New paths have to be searched out. They need change in attitudes and will have to be ready to face hard struggle.

Today country is writhing with pain having trapped in mud of problems. The women will have to come forward to get them relieved. They have to handle the situation. For these achievements there is a great need of perfect education of women.

References

Economic Survey, Different Year (Government of India).
India Today.
Rashtriya Sahara.
Economic and Political Weekly.
Yojna.
Dominion from New Delhi.
Kurukshetra.
Daily Newspapers.

8

The Impact of Social Sector Expansion in a Developing Economy

(With Reference to Indian Economy under Planning)

T.C. PATHAK*

Social sector plays a crucial role in shaping economic forces which in turn have tremendous impact on economic development of a country (Baner, pp. 15-16). The developed countries of Europe and America did not face much of this problem in transforming this sector according to the requirements of the process of economic development. Rather, the process of development itself brought about required changes in social relations, structure and institutions (Meier and Baldwin, pp. 355-59). But the developing countries are facing much of the problems. Their conservative religiously dominated rigidity in social institutions and social structure are not facilitating the transformmation of social sector into a progressive and easily amenable social sector so as to meet the requirements of the

* Formerly, Head of the Economics Department, Government College, Ajmer and Principal (Retd.).

process of development. It rather inhabits this process. Any attempt by such countries as India to develop social sector through expansion of education, medical and health and other facilities has created further problems so that the benefits of development do not reach the masses. This paper attempts to analyse this aspect of the problem with special reference to India.

SPECIFICATION OF THE SOCIAL SECTOR

The social sector is very vast and includes everything relating to human resource—its attitude, size, quality, religious and social beliefs, institutions, etc. which Schumpeter calls "Social Climate", which has a bearing on economic activities under which entrepreneurs must operate (pp. 63-66) and determines risk taking function of an economy. But the analysis of this paper will be confined to two main areas through which social order can be affected. They are education and medical and health care whose importance has been well shown by Summers and Thomas (pp. 245-46). These two areas have been well provided for in various plans in India and the economy has witnessed significant changes in social order.

CLASHING PATTERNS AND DISINTEGRATION OF THE EXISTING SOCIAL ORDER

Much has been talked about the clashing of patterns and disintegration of the existing social order as the economy advances. The existing order in developing countries is based on limited social wants, backward-sloping supply curve of labour and risk taking, aversion to capital and profit, and fatalism and resignation (Bocke, pp. 101-02, 106). But as the economy grows this order is replaced by an order based on unlimited economic wants, always rising supply curve of labour and risk taking, widespread use of capital and prevalence of profit, and finally, a society based on rational human behaviour. This new social order develops as the economy grows through the expansion of education and other social activities. The new social order clashing with the old order creates problems in the short-run till the entire social sector is transformed to new social

TABLE 1

Plan Outlay in Social Sector

(Rs. in crores)

Plan/Item	Education		Health		Family Planning		Housing and urban development		Other social services		Total social services	% of the total plan outlay
	Amount	% share	Amount	% share	Amount	% share	Amount	% share	Amount	% share		
Plan I (1951-56)	149	31.56	98	20.58			129	27.09	96	20.16	472	12.6
Plan II (1956-61)	273	32.76	226	27.12	2	2.4	149	17.88	205	24.60	855	10.4
	(83.22)		(130.61)				(15.50)		(113.54)		(81.14)	
Plan III (1961-66)	661	44.27	226	15.82	25	1.75	128	8.96	453	31.71	1493	10.6
	(142.12)		(00)		(11.50)		(-14.09)		(120.98)		(74.62)	
Annual Plan (1966-69)	354	35.40	140	14.00	71	7.1	73	7.3	338	33.8	976	8.5
Plan IV (1969-74)	905	27.15	336	10.68	278	8.34	270	25.02	1198	35.94	2987	9.6
	(36.91)		(48.67)		(10.12)		(110.94)		(164.46)		(100.06)	
Plan V (1974-79)	1710	34.2	761	15.22	492	9.84	1150	23.00	1904	38.08	6017	7.6
	(88.95)		(126.49)		(76.98)		(325.95)		(58.93)		(101.44)	
Plan VI (1980-85)	2918	18.21	2214	13.81	1448	9.03	2832	17.67	6614	41.27	16026	14.6
	(70.64)		(190.93)		(194.31)		(146.26)		(247.37)		(166.34)	
Plan VII (1985-90)	7685	21.98	3689	10.55	3121	8.93	4835	13.83	15629	44.78	34960	15.8
	(163.36)		(16.62)		(115.54)		(70.72)		(136.30)		(118.14)	
Annual Plans												
1990-91	2063		961		785		1253		4043		9104	
1991-92	2603		1186		749		1748		5504		11790	
1990-95	8473	4.16	3510	2.79	5677	27.45	—	—	—	—	203678	
	(10.25)		(-4.85)		(81.90)						(482.60)	

Sources: Economic Survey, 1984-85 and 1991-92.
Seventh Five Year Plan, 1985-90.
Figures in brackets are % change over previous plan/year. This change for Fourth Plan is over Third Plan.

order conducive to the process of development. In India also same situation prevails even after about 45 years of planning. Through state efforts in the field of education, medical and health etc., the social sector is growing to the new order creating problems not conducive to the success of the development process initiated under planning.

The Expansion of the Social Sector and Human Resource Development

Expansion of the social sector leads to human resource development which in turn affects the size and quality of population. This contributes to economic development of the country. "In these countries, positive population policy may prove to be an essential part of overall planning for economic development (Higgins, p. 687). In India also under planning government adopted a set of measures to develop human resources and followed a population policy. Under this huge amounts of money were spent on different heads of the sector like education, medical and health facilities, housing and urban development, child and woman welfare, etc. This is presented in Tables 1 and 2.

TABLE 2

Central Plan Outlay for Social Sector

(Rs. crores)

Item	*1992-93*	*1993-94*	*1994-95 (BE)*
1. Education	952 (1.96)	1314	1541
2. Health	383 (0.79)	402	578
3. Family Welfare	1190 (2.46)	1523	1430
4. Woman and Child Development	481 (0.99)	573	662
5. Welfare	532 (1.09)	747	705
6. Rural Development	3596 (7.42)	5348	710
Total including others	48,407	63,936	70,141

Source: *Economic Survey*, 1994-95.

Tables 1 and 2 indicate the importance given to the social sector in different plans. The percentage of outlay on social sector to total plan outlay has been between 7.6 to 15.8% in the Seventh Plan. The total amount spent on this sector has grown by as much as 73 times between First Plan (Rs. 472 crores) and Seventh Plan (Rs. 34960 crores). Between different social sectors education and health received highest share and the increase in expenditure on two sectors has been of a very high order.

BASIC INDICATORS OF HUMAN DEVELOPMENT

As a result of the efforts made under planing through expansion of social services, human resource development has taken place bringing about significant changes in size and quality of population. All this information is presented in Table 3.

This table shows that since 1951 declining birth rate and death rate and infant mortality rate has brought at out significant improvement in life expectancy resulting into further increase in population. The rising literacy rate has not yet contributed to decline in birth rate so as to limit the size of population.

EXPANSION OF SOCIAL SECTOR, HUMAN RESOURCE DEVELOPMENT AND ECONOMIC DEVELOPMENT

Expansion of the social sector has had implications for the development of the Indian economy. In the first place the economy witnessed growth rate of around 5% in each Five Year Plan, only recent estimates put it at around 7%. GNP at 1980-81 prices rose from Rs. 42,644 crores to Rs. 4,78,252 crores between 1950-51 to 1990-91 and to Rs. 6,95,342 crores in 1992-93. The increase in population permitted per capita income at 1980-81 prices to rise from Rs. 1127 to Rs. 2178 between the same period and to Rs. 2202 in 1992-93 or by about 95% during the entire 44 years period. This is only 2.16% annual increase in per capital income.

Secondly, inspite all this increase in GNP and per capita income, poverty ratio has remained very high. According to the estimates of the Planning Commission given in Seventh Plan 38.9% of the urban and 50.82% of the rural population remained

TABLE 3

Basic Indicators of Human Development

	Population (In crores)	*Average Annual Growth Rate (%)*	*Birth Rate (Per '000)*	*Death Rate (Per '000)*	*Natural Increase (Per '000)*	*Infant Mortality (Per '000)*	*Life Expectancy at Birth (Yrs.)*	*Literacy Rate (%)*
1941	31.85	1.34	45.2	31.2	14.0			
1951	36.10	1.26	39.9	27.4	12.5	146	32.1	18.3
		(-5.97)	(-11.73)	(-12.18)	(-10.71)			
1961	43.91	1.98	40.9	22.8	18.1	146	41.3	28.3
			(2.51)	(-16.79)	(44.8)	Nil	(28.66)	(54.64)
1971	54.82	2.20	41.1	18.9	22.2	129	45.6	34.5
		(11.11)	(0.49)	(-17.12)	(22.65)	(-11.64)	(10.41)	(21.91)
1981	68.52	2.25	33.3	12.5	20.8	110	50.4	43.6
		(2.27)	(-18.98)	(-33.86)	(-6.31)	(-14.72)	(10.53)	(26.38)
1991	84.63	2.14	29.9	9.8	20.3	80	60.8	52.2
		(-4.89)	(-10.21)	(-21.60)	(-2.40)	(-27.27)	(20.63)	(19.72)
1951-91 (%age)	134.43	59.70	-25.06	64.23	62.40	-45.20	89.41	185.25

Sources: Various Census Reports.
Government of India, Planning Commission, Eighth Five Year Plan, 1992-97, Vol. 1, p. 23, Delhi, 1992.
Economic Survey, 1994-95.
Figures in brakcets are percentage over the previous census year.

below poverty line. This is the biggest challenge to planners. Social sector development must have contributed to economic growth of the economy, but the poverty ratio still remains very high because of the population increase.

Thirdly, expansion of education has raised the literacy ratio substantially, but still it is very low at 52.2%. It also added to educated unemployment which rose from 2.44 lakhs in 1951 to 47 lakhs in 1985 and does not show any sign of reduction. A rise in frustration among the young people is the natural outcome.

CONCLUSION

Expansion of the social sector in India has brought about changes in the human resource through its impact on size and quality of population. With reduced birth rate, death rate and infant mortality rate, and rise in life expectancy due to plan expenditure on medical and health services, child and woman welfare, etc. the size of population has been growing rapidly. Simultaneously, due to improvement in quality of population because of the plan expenditure on education and other factors like investment in productive sectors and infrastructure, the GNP has been rising at about 5% per annum, but because of increase in population rise in per capita income is not very high and poverty ratio though reduced is still high. Similarly, expansion of education has raised literacy ratio but also created the problem of educated unemployment causing frustration among the youth. Consequently, though social sector grows, any substantial improvement in the life of the masses will not take place till adverse effects of social sector expansion are not overcome due to complete change in the outlook of the people and high growth rate achieved by the economy.

REFERENCES

Bauer, P.T., (1957), Economic Analysis and Policy in Underdeveloped Countries, Durham N.C.

Bocke, J.H., (1953), Economics and Economic Policy of Dual Societies, Hoarlem, The Netherlands, Tzeink Willmik.

Higgins, Benjamin (1972), Economic Development, Central Book Depot, Allahabad.

Meier, G.M. and Baldwin, R.E., (1957), Economic Development, John Wiley and Sons, New York.

Schumpeter, A. Joseph, (1969), Theory of Economic Development, Oxford University Press, New York.

Summers, Lawrence H. and Thomas, Vinod (1993), Lessons of Development, World Bank Research Observer, Vol. 8, No. 2, Washington DC.

9

Social Sector and Economic Development in India

PRATIMA TRIVEDI*

Economic development is a very comprehensive term involving various aspects of development. It is very difficult to give one precise meaning to the term economic development. It is a part of one dimension of general development. The concept of economic development has undergone sweeping changes. It is no longer means a process whereby an economy's national income increases over a long period of time. Today economic development is being defined as 'the process of increasing the degree of utilisation and improving the productivity of the available resources of a country which leads to an increase of the economic welfare of the community by stimulating the growth of national income'. From this definition it is clear that the progress of development has to be assessed by reference to indices of production or national income and of economic welfare of the community. While Meier defined economic development as "the process whereby the real per capita income of a country increases over a long period of time subject to the stipulation that the member below an "absolute poverty line"

* Deptt. of Economics, G.N.G.P.G. College, Kanpur.

does not increase and that the distribution of income does not become more unequal".[1]

A rise in per capita income can be deemed development only if it does not increase number of the poor and does not widen income inequalities. A higher per capita income would mean that people are better off and enjoy a higher standard of living, and to raise the level of living of the people is the main objective of economic development. But the increase in national Income or per capita income must be maintained for a long time. A temporary or short-lived increase will not connote real economic growth, because even if the national income goes up, the general standard of living may go down, and this can happen if population of the country is rising more rapidly than the growth of the national income as in India. If it is so, the per capita income falls and we can not call it economic growth.

Thus, a mere increase in per capita income does not necessarily lead to an increase in the welfare of all sections of the people, unless an equitable distribution of the rising product is assured. An equitable distribution is usually taken to mean a reduction in the existing of extreme inequalities in income and wealth distribution may have adverse effect on the economic development of the underdeveloped countries. It has rightly been pointed out by some economists that extreme inequalities in the distribution of income and wealth are detrimental to economic development in so far as they reduce the nutritional wealth and living standards of the people, create an excessive demand for imported luxury consumption goods, further an excessive transfer of funds abroad and prevent the growth of internal markets where such conditions exist fiscal methods are appropriate to bring about more equitable distribution of incomes and channel additional resources into economic development.[2] Besides extreme inequalities create political and social discontent, generate instabilities and as a result, the process of economic development.

Previously the physical capital (like construction, machinery, etc.) was usually taken as the determinant of economic development. In most of the theories and models, growth is directly related only to the physical capital. Gradually the importance of human capital in economic development is felt and economic development is considered in terms of social well being, social justice and richer social life involving good health and education. In the last stage social expenditure was considered to productive expenditure and will directly help in the development of physical aspect. Social capital is not only productive but determine the efficiency and productivity of physical sector.

In an underdeveloped country like India, the process of human capital formation implies the development of abilities and skills of people. It involves investment in human beings to make them more productive which helps in the development of physical capital of the country. During the development process, a nation has to absorb new technology and develop the productive apparatus.

In economic terminology human capital defines people as a capital asset which helps in country's production and yields a stream of economic benefits over their working life. Human capital can be increased by a number of ways. Generally, the investment in human capital is restricted to two types of expenditure, i.e. Education and Health. The expenditure on education includes general education which improves mental capacity of people and other one is technical training that helps in their working capacity to produce more and thus increasing the production of the country. The second one is expenditure on the provision of health facilities which includes health care services and medical education to maintain the health facilities. The health items increases directly the physical capacity of human beings, i.e. the producing factor. The capital aspect of the quality of human beings by improvement in education, training and health, etc. also turn as a consumer good, because it gives them a mean to enjoy life fully in a respectful social setup. Thus the formation of human capital has a dual function, a producer good as well as a consumer good.

HUMAN CAPITAL: A BOOM TO ECONOMY

Human capital has a big importance in the growth of the economy. In some type of industries there is no alternative but to use more of capital. These are aircraft, manufacture, petroleum, chemicals etc. But there are many other industries where alternative technologies are available and in respect of which decisions in favour of labour intensive industries could be made. In fact, in case of some products, India already had such labour absorbing technologies such as manufacture of cloth, leather products, edible oil, rice and wheat husking, bread-making, utensil making, glass factories etc. In the production of these labour absorbing goods, the labour with better skill and higher capacity for work directly adds to production.

A country's productive capacity largely depends on the natural resources available without a minimum availability of natural resources, it is idle to expect any sizable economic growth. But the existence of natural resources is not a sufficient condition of economic growth. As in India, abundance of natural resource is here, yet it is poor and underdeveloped, because the natural resources have not been properly harnessed and fully exploited. Hence, availability of natural resources by itself cannot bring about economic development. Ability to utilise them is also required. The supply of natural resources can be increased by research and technological process which helps in the discovery of new resources (e.g. oil resources in India) and putting to economical use of resources which have been lying useless, and the shortage of some can be made good by synthetic materials. The use of natural resources and their contribution to economic development has a close connection with the type and level of technology.

In India, where physical capital is scarce and labour is abundant, innovations in the equipment and practices relating to work, i.e. Research and Development is an important factor which influences the growth of the economy. As rightly opined by Dr. Rao, "In a country like India, where labour constitutes the dominant element among the factors of production and there is scarcity of capital, human capital becomes even more significant in analysing economic growth".[3] In India, Research and Development expenditure as 'a proportion of the Gross National Produce (GNP) is extremely low and has continuously been declining since 1988-89. The proportion peaked at 0.96% in 1988-89 and was 0.83% in 1992-93. Most of the R & D expenditure is by the Government and the public sector. There are 1,230 in house centres in Indian industry and R & D expenditure incurred by these is around Rs. 1,300 crore (1993-94). The share of the public Sector is 45% and that of the private sector is 55%. R & D expenditure by the in-house centres as percentage of ' their annual turnover is only 0.57% that of the private sector is 0.64% and the public sector's is 0.51%. The private firms are showing some initiatives but it is not enough. The South Korean Government, during industrialisation pushed the responsibility of R & D on individual firms. South Korea today has the largest expenditure on R & D among developing countries, i.e. 2% of its GNP. Developing countries need to assimilate the advances in production methods and management for the sake of improving the quality and quantity of their growth. Hence it is imperative that adequate provision be made for incorporation of such knowledge in human bodies.

Hence, for the dynamic growth of the economy and to make it useful from the social welfare point of view. It is necessary to invest in Human Resource Development (HRD). The aim of economic, social and political stability can be achieved only with a strong social infrastructure. A nation's multi-sided development depends on the development of social sector of the country. The development is not possible without co-existence of physical and social progress. The expansion of social infrastructure helps to remove the barriers of economic development and also helps in the better use of resources. Economic development gets fast with the development of moral values, education, health and training, etc. Trained and skilled labour power directly increases the productivity of the country. The investment in HRD also increases job opportunities in the country.

An optimum utilisation of physical resources and technological capital is possible only due to the development of social sector and due to better technology and highly trained healthy human power with high moral values. There is a possibility of misuse of physical capital in the absence of trained and skilled labour which may decrease the productivity of the country. The distribution system of a country also improves with the development of social sector. Labour power of higher quality gets proper remuneration and there are less possibilities of exploitation of healthy and educated citizens because they are much aware of their rights. Thus social sector on the one hand helps in country's development and on the other it helps in equitable distribution system which is must for legitimate growth of the country. Another advantage of social sector development is, scientific and technological quality improves due to highly educated and trained human resources and it proves fruitful to increase production and multi-sided development of the country. Better health and better education develops the feeling of self-confidence among human beings so that they became responsible and perform their duties more carefully.

Now it is clear that education and health both are very important factors of human capital. Today all the development experts accepted the correlation of education and economic development. That is why developed countries are spending a large amount on the development of education. According to World Development Report, 1995, the pescentage of Government Expenditure on education of various countries is as following:

Singapore—22.3%, France—7.7%, India—2.2%, Ghana—22.0%, Pakistan—1.1%, Srilanka—10.5%, Indonesia—10.0%, Phillipines—15.9%, Rumania—9.0%, Tunisia—17.5%,, Thailand—21.1%, Chekoslovakia—11.0%, Malaysia—20.3%, Korea—16.1%, New Zealand—14.1%, Australia—7.2%.

In the above table one thing is to be noticed that the percentage expenditure on education varies according to their population, size of the budget and the share of responsibility of Central Government in education. It doesn't show the clear picture of education in highly developed countries as in England—3.3%, Canada—2.7%, America—2.0% and in Germany—0.18%. The percentage may be high according to the different circumstances and conditions of living In these countries.

In India there is an urgent need to improve quality as well as quantity of education and to pay proper attention in this area. The present position in respect of the development of human resources does indicate some progress in this field. This may be described in terms of the changes and improvements in the education and health, the two major elements of human capital formation.

LITERACY AND EDUCATION

Our education system is being considered as the most important aspect of development of human capital. The number of educational institutions has increased by more than three times from 2.31 lakhs in 1951-52 to more than 7.87 lakhs in 1988-89. In this field, the expansion has taken place at all the levels, i.e. primary, middle and high/higher secondary, college, professional Institutions and Universities. These Institutions cater in various courses and skills, namely arts, commerce, science, engineering, technology, medicine, etc. The number of primary schools increased from 2.10 lakhs in 1950-51 to 5.81 lakh in 1994-95. During the same period the number of upper primary schools rose from 0.13 lakh to 1.63 lakh. The Gross Enrolment Ratio (GER) in the primary stage increased from 42.6 percent in 1950-51 to 103 percent in 1994-95 and upper primary stage from 12.7 per cent to 65.5 per cent. As a result of this expansion, Indian elementary education has became one of the largest education systems in the world, providing access to schools within one Km. of walking distance to 8.25 lakh habitations covering 94% of the country's population. This has contributed to rise in the overall literacy rate at 52.2 per cent (of the population 7 years and above) in 1991 as compared to 18.3 per cent in 1951. Besides, Kerala has attained the distinction of a state with hundred per cent literacy.

As a result the national stock of educated man-power has increased by as much as twelve times from under 4 million in 1950-51 to about 48 million in 1984-85. In this respect India ranks third in the world. The National Literacy Mission (NLM) has been mandated to make 100 million persons literate in the age group of 15-35 by the end of the Eighth Five Year Plan. The total literacy campaign has become the principal strategy of the NLM in the eradication of illiteracy throughout the country. As on December 1995, 368 districts have been covered under the total literacy campaigns, either fully or partially. Similarly, 157 districts have also been covered under the post-literacy campaigns. Under all schemes of NLM, 49.89 million persons have so far been made literate as per NLM norms an enrolment of 78 million.

As far as the allocation of funds is concerned, the central plan allocation for education was raised from Rs. 952 crore in 1992-93 to Rs. 1825 crore in 1995-96. Primary and adult education have proportionally higher share in the increased allocation. These shifts in inter-sectoral prior in allocation are in the right direction and have direct relevance to the poor. The share of the government in financing educational institutions has been very high. In 1989-90, it accounted for about 93.41 per cent of total income of educational institutions whereas the share from fees and endowments and other sources of educational institutions declined sharply. In 1950-51 the share of fees was 20.39%, in 1980-81 it was 8.20% while in 1989-90 it declined to 3.55%. The share of endowments and other sources was 11.62% in 1950-51, it was 4.03% in 1980-81 while it declined to 3.04% in 1989-90.

MEDICAL AND HEALTH CARE

In respect of Medical and Health facilities. Something has been achieved in this sphere. There is a considerable increase in the number of medical institutions. The number of medical colleges has increased from 28 in 1950-51 to 128 in 1991 and 146 in 1992-93. This figure remain the same till 30th June 1995. The number of dental colleges has gone up from 4 to 40 during the same period. Hospitals and dispensaries too have increased in number. Hospitals from 2,614 in 1951 to 111,174 in 1991 while in the number of dispensaries from 6515 in 1951 to 27,431 in 1991. The number of registered medical practitioners has increased substantially from about 60,000 in 1951 at about 3,20,000 in 1988-89 and 4,10,875 in 1992-93. The number of registered nurses too has gone up from 16,550 in 1951 to 3,40,208 in 1991-92 and 4,49,351 in 1993-94. As a result of this expansion in health facilities, there is an improvement in the health status of the people. The life expectancy of birth has increased from 32.1 years in 1950-51 to 59 years in 1989-90. While the rate of infant mortality has declined from 146 per thousand in 1951 to 95 in 1989-90. There is a considerable reduction in the incidence of communicable diseases also. Specific efforts have also been made to promote the Indian system of Medicine because of its traditional acceptance by the population and local availability of personnel belonging to these systems. A committee has been set up by the Planning Commission to comprehensively review the existing public health system in India and suggest measures for its improvement.

OTHER SIDE OF THE COIN

Despite large quantitative expansion the facilities are still very short of the needs. There are a number of weaknesses in our education health Scenario. As far as Education is concerned it has a very narrow coverage of the entire population of the country with a low retention rate. At the level of primary and secondary education, there are so many children in the age group of 6 to 14 do not attend classes. If 100 children entering Class I, only 37 make it to the end of Class Vth. In respect of primary education about 17% of females remain outside the educational mainstream. As far the secondary education, the situation is bad to worse, about 59 per cent of children do not enrol themselves and 71% of females remain without education. Among those who join these institutions there are large dropouts, less than 3% complete Class XII. The extremely poor retention rate at the primary level has been traced to the general negligence of the sector, while looking at the cost of education, the expenditure on higher education has crowded out the growth of primary education because it has high unit cost defined as the percentage of per capita GNP spent on each pupil ranges from 6 for primary education to 231 for higher education. Despite, the quality of the education is low and the content less relevant to the needs of the individual and the society. Moreover, there is little that has been achieved in respect of literacy for the illiterate. The total literacy rate is 52.2% (male 64.1% and female 39.3%) which is still far off the 100% mark.

In the Fourth World Women's Conference held in Beijing in Sept. 1995, the first commitment (out of five distinct commitments made by India) was 'To increase investment on education to 6 percent of the GDP with major focus on women and the girl child'. It was a plan of having full literacy by the year 2005 with the share of expenditure on education to reach 6 percent of GDP by the year 2000. But in the budget (1996-97) the plan allocation for the department of education has increased substantially from Rs. 1,825 crore to 3,888 crore with a focus on the implementation of the district primary education programme and mid-day meal scheme and no special mention is made to 'women' and 'girl child' as highlighted in the country's statement made in the Beijing conference.

The position respecting Health Facilities is not better too. The population per physician is about 2,520 in India, while in advanced countries the population per physician is 470 (in U.S.A.) and 660 (in Japan). So is the case of nursing person. In India the population per nurse is 1,700 while it is 70 in U.S.A. and 180 in Japan. There is also acute shortage of beds in Hospitals only 82 beds for one lakh of population.

Regarding public hygiene, as drinking water, drainage and sanitary arrangements are woefully inadequate. In case of serious diseases there is very little of efforts at preventive measures. Most of the developing countries are facing same problems. "Drinking water is in short supply in about 80 developing countries and the problem is likely to get far worse in the next few decades as population levels increases", experts said at a five day conference held in Berlin in May 1996 by the 'German Foundation for International Development'. Around 50 international experts took part and discussed more effective ways of using water and supplying clean drinking water. It was reported that about 40 per cent of the world's population live in the 80 countries with the most serious water problems. Four out of five illness in these countries are caused by dirty water. These developing countries are neither in a position to supply clean drinking water nor water to meet the rising demands of agriculture and industry.

The second commitment of Beijing World Women's Conference was 'Universalisation of mother and child care programme to reach out to every corner of the country.' The reach of the programme concerning health of women in our country is not up to the mark. India's material mortality rates in rural areas are among the world's highest and it does not speak of a very healthy and integrated health programme. Only in 'Phulbani' (Orissa) out of 100 pregnant women 75 die during pregnancy and 5% of women do not have any type of medical facility at the time of delivery. Infectious diseases, malnutrition and maternal and pre-natal causes account for most of the disease burden. Although child mortality has declined significantly over the past two decades, over 30 percent of all deaths in India occur among children under five and also the child mortality rates are more for girls than boys.

It is a good news that National Policy for the Empowerment of women has finally been drafted but it took the Government 45 years to realise that it had not been able to protect the rights of women to ensure their educational, political and economic empowerment despite provisions in the constitution. The National Policy stresses gender sensitisation programme which promote education for women's equality and not so much for equalisation of educational opportunities. It seeks to establish an education system which would play an interventionist role in the empowerment of women. The policy also notes that women have to be empowered to fight against physical and mental injustice. The policy is infact good but the actual test will be when it is implemented. If there is a political will to empower women, this is the time to prove it. In India, circumstances differ from other developing countries. Thus here, women need a post-Beijing Development agenda that will constitute a charter for action, one which will; seek to reverse the feminisation of poverty, and lead Indian women's voices in expressing their hopes and aspirations for equality, peace and a healthy environment to live in. But we must shake off the old habit of taking one step forward and two steps backward. Only the making of programmes and policies is not enough, their proper implementation is must for the overall development of the country.

Notes and References

1. Gerald, M. Meier, 'Leading Issues in Economic Development, (1984).
2. 'Methods of Financing Economic Development', p. 15, UN Department.
3. Rao, V.K.R.V., 'India's National Income, 1950-1980'.
4. Human Development Reports, 1990, 1993, 1995.
5. World Development Report, 1995.
6. *Economic Survey*, 1995-96.

10

Planning for Developing Countries: An Egalitarian Approach

MUKUL SRIVASTAVA*

During the two decades following the Second World War economic planning in less developed countries became highly fashionable. By 1970 there hardly existed a developing country, without some kind of development plan. Pearson *et al* (1969)[1] is of the opinion that usually these plans prepared at the urging of and the technical assistance from the international aid agencies and western donors, these documents aspired to set a highly ambitious targets, predicted on the expectations of generous forging aid funds from western resources. For their part Western aid givers were motivated by multiplicity of objectives, partly humanitarian, partly commercial and partly military in nature. Regarding the initiation of efforts for centralised planing ward (1974)[2] and Ranis (1972)[3] write that the dominant rationalisation was the 'WIDENING GAP' theory. Its central argument was that while the advanced, industrialised countries of west were attaining higher standards of living, the under developed countries of the Third World were becoming poorer.

Model-building was the indispensable tool of planners

* Lecturer, Deptt. of Social Work, Institute of Social Sciences, Agra.

and economists involved in the design of development plans. Models afforded the means for he application of economic theories to the practical task of the planning. The typical development plan in the early post-war period was a macro-model based on certain key aggregate relationships between employment, output and investment. The UN took the initiatives and in ECAFE (1955)[4] it was argued than the rate of economic growth may be analytically considered as being the function of two factors: (a) the rate of capital formation, and (b) the capital-output ratio; accordingly development policies may be described aiming to increase the rate of capital formation, reduce the capital-output ratio or do both.

Macro models were logically, complete constructions designed for internal consistency. The need of consistency was obvious: to avoid resource bottlenecks or surpluses in the process of growth. The Indian planning experience based on a 'grand strategy' is a good example of macro-model building. This strategy was heavily influenced by macro-economic theories involving the two important dimensions suggested by Mahalanobis (1955).[5] These models considered the theories of sequential Inter-Industry flows and optimal timing. The basic Mahalanobis idea was that the growth process should be carefully integrated and the growth of each sector phased overtime to achieve optimal sectoral linkages and interdependence. Thus, the first sector to be developed was heavy industry centred around the creation of an Indian iron and steer industry. This was necessary to increase the domestic supply of producer goods which subsequently would be needed to develop consumer goods industries.

Lewis (1954)[6] observes that Western economics is characterised by a fundamental split between two major themes: efficiency in production and equity in the distribution of products. The principle of efficiency, derived from the notion of a rational 'economic man' with limited funds facing a perfectly competitive market operating according to Adam Smith's famous 'invisible hand' doctrine ensures in theory that scarce resources are utilised in their most profitable uses. The pursuit of profit maximization may create income differentials amongst citizens or it may cause unequally distributed opportunities, but there are deemed necessary indeed desirable in order to act as incentives in the form of rewards and penalties, for promoting a level of aggregate out put which is both the largest possible and rapidly growing.

Yet, these same differentials violet the principles of equity, derived from humanistic and egalitarian traditions proclaimed in constitutional and political institutions guaranteeing universally distributed rights, privileges to all individuals. The most efficiently working market place may result in a degree of deprivations and poverty that conflicts with such basic human values as dignity equality and fairness. The ultimate test for any process of social and economic development is that it should serve both the efficiency and equity objectives. At many points along the growth path, these two objectives may conflict with each other. For example, anti-poverty programmes desired to shift income to the low income groups to reduce income inequalities may also tend to weaken the incentives for investment and growth. However, the equity and efficiency are not necessarily always conflicting. This is especially so in most developing countries with large volumes of unemployed or underemployed labour force, potentially available for productive utilisation that would both increase the level of national output and the income share of the poor.

In the planning in developing countries, a most unfortunate strategy choice was made usually with active encouragement of the international financial institutions: equity was sacrificed for the sake of efficiency. Equitable income distribution, while generally acknowledged as a desirable objective was traded for the immediate goal of maximising the gross national product. In the process, there was no point in becoming concerned about distribution, when there was practically nothing to distribute. It was essential to postpone or delay equity considerations until some more favourable situations arise.

Haq (1971)[7] comments that the planning trade off in favour of efficiency was responsible for what has been described as 'hot pursuit in GNP'. The evidence now accumulating and analysed clearly demonstrate that the preoccupation with efficiency objectives has been a failure. To be sure, industrialisation has helped to attract multinationals in modern sectors, utilising western investments and techniques of production. But only in rare cases did industrialisation lead to the general improvement in the living standards of the majority of inhabitants. Usually, growth of GNP has been accompanied with greater income concentration in the top layer of the socio-economic pyramid with mass poverty at bottom.

ECONOMIC GROWTH, SOCIAL JUSTICE AND EGALITARIAN DEVELOPMENT

A process of economic growth which worsens social and economic inequalities is elitist and morally indefensible. It is growth without equity. It is against the ideals of social and distributive justice, which are broader in scope than the concept of political justice. Social justice proclaims the idea of a fair distribution of economic and social benefits as well as costs. Robertsons (1972)[8] writes that concept of social justice has been derived from historical egalitarian principles and typically enshrined in the constitutions of so many nations as well as in the United Nations Declaration of Universal Human Rights and other conventions. The search for social justice has been a driving force behind man's long struggle for a better life for all.

Mishan (1964)[9] comments that the 'dismal sciences' of economics is ·by no means silent on the subject of social justice. The general normative guidelines of social justice for economic policy can be derived from the axioms of welfare economics. This for example is the idea behind the famous compensation principle formulated by a number of welfare economists such as Kaldor, Hicks, Little and Stavosky. According to this doctrine, an economic policy measure, which met the efficiency conditions, would be judged socially justified on equity grounds as well if it increased the standard of living of the underdeveloped by harming on one. However, if there occurs a welfare loss for some individuals, while benefiting others, than the gainers ought to be potentially capable of compensating the losers.

Nevertheless, there is a strong presumption that the interests of the losers should be safeguarded in some appropriate way. This fact is emphasised in the theory of justice as fairness advanced by Rawls (1971).[10] His conception of justice rests on two basic principles: the first requires equality in the assignment of basic rights and duties, while the second holds that social and economic inequalities, for example, in equalities of wealth and authorities are just only if they result in compensating benefits for everyone and in particular for the least advantaged members of the society.

Regrettably, the concept of social justice had no practical relevance in the process of growth and development in most developing countries. This does not mean that the planning objectives totally ignored egalitarian ideals: on the contrary, national plan documents almost always contained long and ambitious lists of promises, necessary for promoting social justice. But these were largely for ideological purposes.

Indian Planning Commission (1961)[11] expressed similar objectives of social justice. Ever since the Independence, two main objectives have guided India's planned development—to build up democratic means, a rapidly expanding and technologically progressive economy and a social order based on justice and offering equal opportunity to every citizen. The nation aspires to a standard of living for all its people as high as can be achieved with the resources available to it; equitable distribution of wealth; education to all in accordance with their talents; victory over disease; adequate facilities for transportation and communication so that the nation may be effectively unified economically and socially.

These and similar lofty aims were abandoned during the implementation and execution stages of plans. This happened mainly because the elite management of planning and policy in developing countries. Elites generally control the political system and the economic planning as well decision-making machinery of these countries. These elites were successful in influencing the allocation of planned investment expenditures and channelling them into the programmes to safeguard their own interests, wealth, status and power.

Radianive (1966)[12] observes that the income concentration at the top socio-economic stratum was achieved through a growth strategy that actively encouraged the expansion of property income at the expense of employment income. Property income accrues primarily to asset holding groups, such as landlords, industrialists and owners of fixed capital and cash balances. These asserts earn dividends, interest, rent and other forms of properly income. Employment income on the other hand, accrues to wage and salary earners. Since the growth in low developing countries was based on capital intensive industrialisation, it seriously limited the growth of jobs and income employment while the priority accorded to capital formation greatly enhanced the share of property income. In the view of the fact that wealth assets are heavily concentrated at top, it follows that income maximization through industrialisation in developing countries is a process creating greater inequalities.

The experience gained regarding the abuses of economic planning and policy in developing countries by the elites, can and should serve as a valuable guide for future action to promote social justice.

This chapter advocates the concept of egalitarian planning as a tool for levelling incomes, expanding employment and meeting the basic needs of the bulk of the populations. Some of the basic elements of egalitarian planning are based on a decentralised pro-rural approach. Central to our discussion is the assumption that the price market system reinforced by reformist and progressive intervention in the economic and planning process, is quite competable with egalitarian approach. What we wish to do is to formulate the broad outlines of a feasible economic and social development strategy which would be capable of delivering substantially greater income security and other benefits to the majority of population. In the words of Rescher (1974)[13] we wish to make development planning an egalitarian tool so that planning promotes not income concentration but social justice, serving the needs of all groups of population.

ECONOMIC GROWTH AND DEVELOPMENT

There is a difference between the concept of growth and development. The former is a narrower idea and refers to the expansion of national income or production most typically measured as GNP or GDP per capita, as a result of increased capital formation and input utilisation. On the other hand, the idea of 'development' is much broader in cope and refers to a general improvement in the material and social well being of the society as a whole.

Myrdal (1964)[14] describes that general improvement incorporates high income per capita and also requires reforms in institutional or quasi-economic framework such as wider accessibility to education, health and welfare facilities, greater political participation in the national decision-making process and a more equitable distribution benefits of progress achieved through economic planning.

Baran (1957)[15] comments that the reasoning behind the distinction between growth and development is essentially based on a fundamental difference between the rate and pattern of economic charge. Statistically, a developing country may achieve an impressive GNP growth; yet growth may reflect an uneven pattern with the mass of the population receiving marginal benefits or even being harmed, while a tiny privileged at the top increases its wealth and power.

The clear implication is that development requires reforms designed to bring about an open society based on equality of opportunity in labour markets, equal access to quality education and training, balanced regional and rural growth and generally a more equitable distribution of wealth and incomes.

Egalitarian Development: Some General Assumption

The concept of egalitarian development in developing countries does not call for perfect equality for every one in consumption or living standards. The focus attention is on the elimination of excessively large disparities between different individuals, groups and regions. In short, egalitarian development is a plea to make economic planning and policy an anti-poverty tool. Atkinson (1975)[16] explains egalitarian planning as a strategy that would tend to equalise living standards without necessarily leading to perfect equality as the final result.

For budgetary and administrative reasons, excessive disparities in income and living standards between individuals can not be minimised overnight. This task must begin urgently but proceed in orderly manner within the framework of priorities. The first and foremost important is the equalisation of consumption of basic needs such as foods, shelter and clothing. Equally important is the equalisation of opportunities or assess *vis-a-vis* the supply of public goods and services, such as education, health and welfare. Of critical importance is the necessity of institutional and administrative reforms in the governmental and political framework in order to ensure the execution of an equitable distribution pattern.

Rawls (1971)[17] suggests the following guidelines for the egalitarian planning for developing countries:

1. production and consumption of goods and services must be for the common goods and satisfy both efficiency and equity criteria,
2. anti-poverty planning and policy instrument should be utilised to eliminate excessively large disparities in income and living standards between individuals, groups and regions, and
3. The political decision-making process must be reformed to permit people participation, so that social choice reflect the needs and preferences of all social groups.

These basic guidelines of Rawls are based on the utilitarian principle of the 'greatest good of greatest possible number'.

The egalitarian approach recognises the effective and rational organisation of production in most efficient feasible manner on one hand and that every member of the society has a valid claim to a share of the total output on another hand. This share need not to be equal share, specially in view of differentiation of economic roles and occupational specialization, but it should be a just or fair share defined according to some ethical norms or economic principle (i.e., equal pay to equal work) relative to a particular area.

The magnitude of disparities in consumption and living standards in developing countries is so large that the introduction of egalitarian, anti-poverty planning measures can and should be started without any delay, wherever feasible.

Egalitarian Pattern of Consumption

Consumption is the ultimate objective of all production. The notion of production of goods and services for the 'common goods' is a recognition of the value judgement that it should enhance the well being of all, rather than merely of certain groups.

Equalisation of Consumption of Basic Needs

Regardless of difference in rank, status and income basic want in terms of food, shelter and clothing, medical care, essential for the healthy survival of individual are remarkably uniform for every human being, although, of course their are differences in food intake housing, clothing and health requirements due to climatic and environmental conditions and factors. There are many problems of measurement in the estimation of poverty lines or minimum consumption levels. Nevertheless, for many developing countries deficiencies in basic human needs are so propounded and disparities in living standards between the 'haves' and 'have nots' so wide that policies designed to reduce these disparities are urgently required. The argument that developing countries are too poor to undertake such redistributive measure, is hardly acceptable in view of the severe wealth and income concentration at the top.

It is most important to emphasise, that the intention of egalitarian approach to planning implies that there should be both minimum as well maximum level of income. While this double requirement is a relatively radical reform, it is logically and practically unavoidable if there is to be a progressive redistribution from the rich to the poor. For, if only minimum level of income is imposed, there would be no assurance that overtime there would not be concentration at top.

It is evident that implementing any redistributive measure to minimise excessively large disparities in consumption and living standards would cause some welfare loss for elites. But to the extent that egalitarian reforms are financed out of future income growth, there losses need only affect relative distribution without requiring absolute reduction in the current wealth position of the rich. Additionally, if social investment in health, education and rural development effectively raised the productivity of land and labour both equity and efficiency objectives would be served. Pigoue (1951)[18] writes that the proposition of equalising consumption of basic needs can be justified on both subjective and objective grounds. One of the central theorems of economic theory is the Law of Diminishing Marginal Utility of Money Income, which is a reflection of the act that one extra rupee confers more welfare or utility to a poor person than to a rich person and that therefore a rupee transferred from a rich to a poor person would increase the aggregate welfare, since the incremental loss suffered by a rich person if more than offset by the poor persons incremental gain. This is the fundamental justification for income transfer programmes and social security scheme in industrial countries. The second principle is the imperially testable fact of Income Inelasticity of Demand for Food Items. There are evidences supported by studies that the proportion of income spent on food stuffs declines as the level of income rises, which suggest that the rich and poor consumers differ more in terms of consumption of luxury items than in terms of basic needs. These two theoretical frameworks warrant the introduction egalitarian approach for planning in developing countries.

Public Goods and Luxuries

Since egalitarian approach is not concerned with perfect equality of consumption levels between individuals, certain difference must be reckoned with. These difference are most likely to emerge from variability in human talents, preferences and capacities for whatever reasons and they would ordinarily be revealed in terms of consumption of non-essential goods and services. In the case of public goods and services such as education, transport and communication for example the egalitarian requirements would be that every one should have an equal opportunity or access to for the enjoyment of such goods and services. In the case of education no one ought to be denied. Schooling opportunity in the line with his abilities and desire for lack of necessary means. These propositions have important implications for taxation and subsidy programmes as well as for the regional development. In the case of primary luxury consumer goods, consumption should be subject to progressive taxation based on ability to pay.

Egalitarian Production

So far we have been concerned with the consumption. No system of egalitarian development can ignore the vital importance of production of goods and services. After all there must be production in order to satisfy human needs and wants.

Distribution *versus* Redistribution

It will be useful to start with the important distinction between distribution and redistribution. The latter can be defined as income transfers between the individuals, at a constant level of aggregate income (assuming that a rupee has equal value for every one). This is also known as Zero Sum Game. In this zero sum game, income shares would necessarily change. Distribution, however, may or may not alter the income shares, because it is associated with increased income. Additional income may be allocated according to the old sharing pattern, or a new one. In usual case, egalitarian reforms would be financed out of additional income with a greater share going to the lower income group. In the case land reforms however redistribution of ownership is unavoidable.

Rewards and Incentives

Baumol (1967)[19] rationally comments in his writings that the pursuit of egalitarian objectives in consumption needs to be counter balanced with some schemes of rewards and incentives that does not unduly harm productive enterprise and private initiative. The concept of egalitarian development is not to be equated with the absolute levelling of socio-economic differences. Human nature, as revealed in terms of abilities, preferences, and expectations, is too diverse to permit perfect standardisation. It is required to utilise economic planning and policy in developing countries as tools for enabling every one, and not a privileged minority, to enjoy the benefits of modern technology.

In this context there is no necessary conflict between the objective of efficient production and private initiative and rewards. Socio-economic differentiation is not inconsistent with human nature. The important principle of equity is that every person ought to have equal opportunity for economic security, education and self-development, providing only that it precludes excessive income and wealth accumulation.

Conflicting Interests

Undoubtedly, egalitarian policies do often entail conflicts of interests between the various social, political and economic groups. Any redistribution of assets benefiting the low income recipients would require a corresponding loss for the rich; likewise a nationalisation, without compensation, would clash with the interests of the groups at top. These conflicts, however, arise from legal, political or institutional factors rather than from conflicting technical or economic efficiency criteria. To the extent that egalitarian development entails 'Zero Sum Game' in which losses and gains always add up to zero the groups suffering losses can be expected to resist redistributive measures and reforms. OKUN (1977)[20] comments in this connection that the maximum limits on excessive wealth and income level proposes, would be resisted strongly by rich elites, while firms accustomed to any scheme of profit squeeze. The seriousness of elite resistance to egalitarian reform should not be underestimated. For, although numerically small, elites control the political and government machinery and this control is of fundamental importance both in general terms and particularly for the formation and conduct of economic policy. Thus the ruling elites would be capable of mobilising, if and when deemed necessary the following:

(a) they might cut down the flow of private and public investment expenditure, causing stagnation and employment.

(b) they could impose the direct or indirect restrictions on wages, employment income and consumption through fiscal, monetary or commercial policies.

It is almost certain that the social and economic hardship caused by such negative measures would fall on the poor, marginal and weak sections of the society and not on the privileged and affluent groups. The root cause of this situation is that the apparent trade off between maximum rate of growth of production and equitable distribution are social legal and political, emanating from institutional ownership of resources rather than from technical constrains. Hence it is important to note that the resolution of the trade off problems must be sought primarily in the political decision making process, rather than in price market theory.

Instruments of Egalitarian Development

If economic planning is to work as an egalitarian tool, it must aim at increasing the income share of the poor and marginal groups. Operationally, this implies that economic planning must satisfy the needs of these groups. But there are certain important questions to be answered. What most efficient or appropriate strategy to respond to these needs? What about the price market mechanism can it play a role, any role, in the promotion of egalitarian objectives?

To begin with the last question, a system of rewards and incentives is an essential element of egalitarian production. The price market system, by itself may fail to bring about a socially optimal pattern of income distribution, but through fiscal policy and other economic measures, it could be reconciled with egalitarian principles. In particular, where the market system tends to concentrate income and wealth in few hands, causing widespread inequality and poverty for others, this tendency can be checked by imposing ceilings on incomes, assets or consumption levels, just with the view that minimum ceiling on incomes would be justified as means of preventing absolute poverty.

On the question of a 'top-down' strategy suggested by Hartcourt (1969),[21] it is evident that there is a hidden assumption that masses perhaps because of illiteracy, are unable or unfit to define their needs in any rational manner; therefore, it would be quite pointless to let them participate in the process of determining planning objectives, priorities and investment choices. This approach which is used by most of the developing countries, fixes the role for planners as deciding, what is good for the masses. This is not only an arrogant approach to development planning, but also plays right in to the hands of powerful elites dominating the political and economic system.

Rather than a top-down strategy of economic planning, we would advocate a fully decentralised approach reaching down to the regional and village level, so that all groups and citizens from all walks of life are given opportunity to participate in the determination of targets, priorities and investment choices reflected in the plans. In this 'bottom up' planning process, the first task of planning is to act as the principal component of state to determine the feasibility of the needs and the requirements of the groups, and regions. Some of the needs may be too ambitious, too costly or based on inappropriate data. If however a meaningful follow upstage were undertaken, in which direct consultation between planners and the affected groups took place, it is certain that there would be considerable progress to minimise the waste and duplication. Nevertheless, it is equally certain that there would be insufficient funds in development budget to even finance the most urgent and basic needs of all groups and regions. Thus the second important role of planners must be the co- ordination of competing claims for limited development resources. Whatever projects are ultimately included in the plans must be justified and fully documented to the satisfaction of the target groups.

Decentralised planning requires a new set of institutions and budgetary and fiscal procedures. In addition to these, it requires effective local government agencies and expended political decision-making. If the decentralised system of planning is actually to be adopted, the masses have to be encouraged to specify their needs and these needs are to be actually incorporated in the plan. But basic question is that what would be some of the typical needs that would be expressed most urgently and extensively? While these needs can be expected to be relative to individual localities, some of most important ones are bound to relate to income security, political, human and legal rights and generally the bread and butter issues of earning decent living. These are the issues with which an egalitarian planning process would be involved. Some of the specific fiscal and economic policy instruments to promote an egalitarian planning and development are to be adopted.

Progressive Taxation

An egalitarian system of public finance would be based on 'ability to pay' and would rely primarily on income tax rather than on indirect forms of taxation. In most developing countries, the share of income tax of total revenue is disproportionately small, while indirect taxes are excessively large and unfairly burdensome for the lower income groups. Richard (1973)[22] comments that this regressive pattern is made worse by extensive tax evasion and avoidance by the affluent and the powerful sanction the society which is the another evidence of elite control of economic political institutions.

Wealth and Inheritance Taxation

In many developing countries elite power and affluence are tied to land ownership and property income. Since wealth and inheritance taxes are generally non-existent or easily avoided by the privileged groups, there is an automatic inter-generational wealth concentration process, in effect creating persistent poverty for the mass and wealth accumulation for the few, growing exponentially overtime. In the past, elites have often successfully resisted land distribution schemes designed to benefit the peasants and they have acquired substantial equity ownership in post-war industrialisation, further adding to wealth, concentration. An egalitarian public finance system would have to include both income consistent with minimum consumption levels and an income ceiling to prevent excessive wealth accumulation. Regarding this Okun (1977)[23] observe that this is not a static problem; it is a dynamic one, since elitist accumulation is tendency which always exists. Excess incomes can be taxed and the proceeds used to finance future redistributive projects.

Public Goods and Regional Balance

The supply of public goods, should in general be in accordance with the egalitarian principle of equal accessibility for all. In the case of housing, health, and welfare as well as educational facilities, there would have to be a balanced regional distribution of facilities and services in order to ensure equality of access for the rural inhabitants. Such a spread of social overhead capital may entail some subsidisation of low income regions at the expense of the regions acting as leading sectors, but this would be fully warranted by social and long-term benefits of an integrated economy.

Public Education

Under egalitarian development strategy, the public education would be guided by the principle of nation-wide equality or educational opportunity. While this would also have the desirable effect of increasing the quality and productivity of manpower resources, educational policy and planning would not be limited to the provision of manpower requirements of growing economy, rather the policy objective would be the development of a nation-wide accessibility to schooling, specially in rural areas to combat illiteracy and ignorance, while increasing the labour productivity for future workers.

Equal Employment Opportunity

Non-discriminatory employment is another important prerequisite of egalitarian development. In developing countries, recruitment of labour involves extensive forms of discrimination. Despite the fact that most countries have legal obligations against the discrimination in employment practice, these are probably the most violated provisions. So long as jobs security persists, it is doubtful that such unfair practices can be stopped and job scarcity can be eliminated only through a deliberate programme of an economic planning and policy that recognise employment creation as the leading objective.

Land Reform

Increased agricultural productivity is an essential precondition of economic development, but agricultural productivity is dependent upon land and labour productivity. Raising land productivity can be accomplished partly through the application of modern agricultural technology. It is also dependent upon the efficient use of the available land. This fact is yet to be fully recognised by the developing country. Land redistribution through effective reform legislation is an essential precondition for raising both productivity of land and labour. For, by providing land and other means of production to landless they can be turned into productive farmers. The alternative method of higher labour productivity, i.e. by pushing large number of migrants into urban factors is a remedy which leads to urban poverty and unemployment.

Social Welfare Functions

Sen (1979)[24] observes that probably the single most important, yet difficult economic task of a political leadership in any of the existing political and economic system, is identifying the ways and means of maximising the aggregate social good. In normative economies this is the problem of specifying a social welfare, i.e. the rules for making fair and efficient social choices.

Specifying a social welfare functions requires not only a strong dedication to justice but also information about the weights to be assigned on the claims of the welfare needs. Under highly restrictive assumption known as Pareto optimum conditions explained by Dobh (1973)[25] this function can be demonstrated in an abstract way that might be possible to have ideal output, optimlly distributed, resulting in maximised collective social welfare.

The central theme of the above discussion is that economic and social development in developing countries in process of change effecting everyone therefore all should be benefited from the result of development achieved.

Developing countries because of their specific basic needs and requirements need egalitarian planning processes, which must be based on the collective social choices and will shift to the requirements of the larger sections of the society. Needless to say, in the world of Bedeau (1979)[26] this approach is based on the assumption that egalitarian planning as a non-violent revolution is both feasible and relevant, given the will to attack the problems of poverty, marginalism, unemployment and unequality.

References

1. Pearson, L.B. *et al*, Partners in Development, Praeger, New York, 1962.
2. Ward, B. *et al* (eds.), The Widening Gap: Development in the 1970's, Columbia University Press, New York, 1971.
3. Ranis, G., (eds.), The Gap Between Rich and Poor Nations, Macmillan, London, 1972.
4. UN, ECAFE 'Economic Development and Planning in Asia and the Far East, *Economic Bulletin for Asia and Far East*, Vol. VI, No. 3 (Nov. 1955) Bangkok.
5. Mahalanobis, C.P., 'The Approach of Operational Research to Planning, Sankhya, Vol. 16, 1965.
6. Lewis, W.A., Economic Development with unlimited supplies of 'Labour', The Manchester School Vol. 22 (May 1954). Reprinted in A.N. Agrawal and S.P. Singh. The Economics under Development, Oxford University Press, New York, 1963.
7. Haq, Mahub ul, Employments in 1970's, A new Perspective, *International Development Review*, Vol. XIII, No. 4, 1971.
8. Robertson, H., Human Rights in the World, Manchester University Press, Manchester, 1972.
9. Mishan, E.J., A Survey of Welfare Economics 1939-1959, *Economic Journal*, Vol. 70, No. 279, reprinted in idems, Welfare Economics Five Introductory Essays, Random House, New York, 1964.
10. Rawls, John, A Theory of Justice, Haward University Press, Cambridge, Mass, 1971.
11. Government of India, Planning Commission, Third Five Year Plan, New Delhi, 1964.
12. Radanive, K.R., Pattern of Income Distribution in India, Bulletin of Oxford University, Institute of Economic and Statistics, 1969.
13. Rescher Nicholas, Distributive Justice: A Constractive Critique of the utilitarian theory of distribution, Blackwell, London, 1974.
14. Marydal Gunner, What is Development, *Journal of Economic Issues*, Vol. 9, No. 4, 1964.
15. Baran Paul, Comments on Clark's Definition of Economic Progress, The Political Economy of Growth, Monthly Review Press, New York, 1964.
16. Atkinson, A.B., The Economics of Inequality, Clarendon Press, Oxford, 1975.
17. Rawls, John, *op. cit*.
18. Pigou, A.C., Some Aspects of Welfare Economics, *American Economic Review*, Vol. XLVI (No. 3), June 1951.
19. Baumol, William J., Welfare Economics and the Theory of State, Harvard University Press, Cambridge, 1979.
20. Okun, M., Equality and Efficiency : A Big Trade Off, The Brookings Institution, Washington DC, 1977.
21. Hartcourt, G.C., 'Some Cambridge Controversies in the Theory of Capital', *The Journal of Economic Literature*, Vol. VII, No. 2, Cambridge, 1969.

22. Richard H. Bird, Taxation and Development, Lesson from Columbian Experience, Harvard University Press, Cambridge, 1973.
23. Okun M., *op. cit.*
24. Sen, A. K., Social Choice Theory : A Re-examination, *Econometrica,* Vol. 45, No. 1, (1977).
25. Dobb, J.N., Welfare Economics, Egalburg Pub. Inc., London, 1973.
26. Bedeau Hugo A., Egalitarianism and the Idea of Equality, Pennok and Chapman, Nomox, 1979.

11

Social Sector and Development: India vis-a-vis SAARC Countries

Harshada S. Rathod*

Services plays a vital role in the democratic economy particularly for developing countries, on account of their inter-linkages with other sectors of the economy. Many service sectors, such as telecommunications and transportation, are a vital part of the infrastructure. Hence, the development of the service sector as a whole plays a big role in the indutrialisation process and contributes to the overall development of developing countries.

The relations between services and development raise an important act of concerns. Firstly, it is misleading to use the terms economic development and economic growth synonymously. While economic growth is usually quantified in terms of the increase in aggregate national income or per capita income, economic development also implies a reduction in poverty, inequality and unemployment and an improvement in living conditions for the majority of the populations. Economic development is not merely a matter of resource allocation based

* Deptt. of Economics, Smt. P.N. Doshi Women's College, Ratan Bang, Cama Lane Ghatkopar (W), Mumbai.

on efficiency; it concerns, perhaps even more fundamentally, the terms and conditions of resource creation, resource mobilisation and resource utilisation.

However, there is a more complex relationship of mutual determination and reciprocal influence between service and development. The service sector satisfies the basic needs in a society through education, health care, income generation, employment creation, etc. It also provide inputs for material production in other sectors, creates an infrastructure to meet national development needs and facilities the development of markets. It contributes to resource mobilistion through financial services to resource utilisation through infrastructural services and to resource creation through technological services.

On the other hand, the stage of development of an economy has a clear impact on the nature and evolution of the service sector. The evolution of the service sector is partly determined by the nature of economic development and influenced by factors such as capital accumulation, technological change, land reform, education and the nature and degree of state intervention.

It is very difficult to give definition of a social service to which one can refer for precise guidance on whether a service is, or is not, a social service. But a social service can be defined as a service provided by the community to help those in need but it need not necessarily, the need of money. The main services are national insurance, social security, health services, educational, legal services, employment services, etc. A state with many statutory social services can be called a welfare state. On the basis of the above brief introduction of importance of services sector an attempt has been made to examine some of the basic social services with reference to SAARC Countries.

One of the main economic objectives of SAARC is to facilitate optimum utilisation of human and material resources, accelerate pace of economic development with the help of free regional trade and investment flows.

The SAARC states are the poorest of poor countries in the world with per capita (GNP according to Human

Development Index 1995, ranging between 5600 (Sri Lanka) with Pakistan ($ 420), Bangladesh ($ 220) and Nepal ($ 170) against the World per capita GNP for the year 1992 of $ 4534. The population of South Asia was estimated at growth of 2.5 per cent during the period 1960-92. The low per capita income and high rates of population growth in SAARC countries have caused lower consumption levels, higher infant mortality rates, illiteracy and lower educational level resulting in poor quality of life (Details are presented in Annexure).

To increase per capita GNP SAARC countries are trying to produce more goods and services, that is, they are trying to make their economics growth. Economic growth depends upon making people increase production by improving their education and health. It also depends upon improving transportation and communication systems, providing between tools and technology, finding reliable sources of energy and increasing access to markets where countries can sell their exports. Many countries are able to use export earnings to develop their economics and per capita GNP rose much faster than the average.

In the current strategic environment the largest throat to our national security is the growing weakness of our economy. In an independent world, it is very difficult for India to develop itself without facing the security problem from the rest of the world like India, most of the third world countries need to feed, house, employ, educate and provide basic health care to their people. Paradoxically, resources are scarce but demands from various quarters, particularly in respect of basic needs are heavy. Consequently, it is very difficult for the developing third world economics to maintain the trend of steady development of its economy without sacrificing some vital national interest. One can generally argue that security expenditure can either promote or kinder economic growth.

An overall picture of the South Asia region which has emerged in the course of time. Since the independence of its nations appears to be very distributing, poverty, population explosion, unemployment, political instability, slow economic growth rate, unequal distribution of wealth, low per capita income, heavy dependence on external assistance are some of the common problems of the SAARC nations. The region is extremely poor in terms of natural resources with exceptions of resources of the Himalayas and sea resources. With small difference, the basic problems of all countries of South Asia are inherently similar and SAARC region are part of this problems. In varying degrees, all of them are under developed, have large masses of their population on the margin of subsistence are failing in keeping pace with the increasing expectations of the people and demands upon their resources and are lacking in the sense of economic and social security for the future.

The countries of the region show wide difference in the Human Development Index. A country like Lanka shows a higher index (.704). Whereas India and Pakistan more than 50 per cent of the index of Sri Lanka, remaining countries are having nearly half of the index, compare to Sri Lanka. In the case of all the developed countries the index is 540 (more than 50 per cent of the world index), whereas in the case of less developed countries it is (index) 1/2 of the world index. But compared to industrial countries, India standard far from that i.e. exactly half of the index of world H.D.I.

The basic feature of SAARC economics even today does not show any significantly change in so far as contribution to the economics of different sectors is concerned. Upto 1987, agriculture continues to play a very dominant role in all these countries. Though the secondary and tertiary sectors are playing a greater role in these economics, the fact remains that agriculture countries to be the single largest sector in all these economics. According to HDI-1995 the picture has changed. Now gradually service sector comes forward and plays a significant role in increasing GDP of a country. It is significant to note that the contribution of agriculture in the countries of South Asia has been reduced, from 45 per cent in 1965 to 34 per cent in 1992. On the other hand, the contribution of industrial sector during the same period has increased from 21 per cent to 23 per cent. The service sector appears to have developed from 35 per cent to 42 per cent which include Bangladesh, Malawai, Pakistan, Sri Lanka and India with contribution of 49 per cent, 50 per cent, 46 per cent, 49 per cent and 40 per cent respectively in the year 1992. In the case of Bhutan and Nepal this sector accounts for about 21 per cent and 30 per cent respectively.

However, the region as a whole is experiencing a high rate of inflation, which has staged at double digit levels in most of the region.

The high rate of population growth neutralise a substantial part of the increase in GDP. The annual growth rate of population in the region in early 1990s was 2.5 per cent compared to an annual growth rate of 1.7 per cent for the world as a whole and a growth rate of .4 per cent for Europe. Population growth makes it difficult to raise standard of living because more people have to be provided, food, energy, housing and health and social services if they want to live healthy productive lives.

Although the health conditions in the region show a remarkable movement, yet the public expenditure on health is very small, not exceeding more than 2 per cent of GNP in most of the nation. Talking about population with access to health services Sri Lanka for better than other countries, while situation of Bangladesh is worst among the SAARC regions. As regards safe water Bhutan gets the last rank, whereas India stands stood at 2nd position. In the case of sanitation facilities also Nepal's and Bhutan's condition is worst compared other countries, while Malawai and Sri Lanka have improved.

The nutritional status of an average Indian is found to be from satisfactory. For capita calorie intake in India is 2395, whereas in the Malawai it is lowest, i.e. 1827.

Poor in adequate nutrition is of the important causes for poor health in these countries causing inefficiency among people. Supply of medical personnel may helpful in improving health conditions. In this case, Sri Lanka stands at a better position followed by India and Malawai. Poor inadequate nutrition and health services is one of the important causes of poor reproductive health in these countries.

Talking about life expectancy India is still lagging behind compared to Sri Lanka and Pakistan, where it is above 61 years, while the position of Malawai is the last (45.6 years). The high rate of infant and child deaths is one of the main reasons why life expectancy is low in other countries. Drinking water is often impure and sanitary conditions are common. Pregnant women, nursing mothers, infants and children may not get enough nutritious food. Government and families often can not afford adequate health care. Many children are not immunised against polio, measles, diphtheria, etc. Therefore, expectancy for people of all ages is lower in Malawai, Bhutan, Nepal and Bangladesh. Average life expectancy in the world rise from 58 years in 1965 to 65.7 years in 1992. Much of this increase reflects the fact that, as countries develop economically and living conditions improve, more infants survival in the first years of life.

The adult literacy rate in Sri Lanka has increased to 89.3 per cent, whereas India is still behind, i.e. 49.9 per cent, while in Nepal it is found to be lowest, i.e. 25.6 per cent. This indicates that India is carrying on with a large number of illiterate adults. Educational opportunities are still not equal. Particularly girls in rural areas, where fewer than half of the girls of secondary school age are enrolled in schools.

Therefore, countries need more money to continue improving the quality of basic education. This also suggests that special programmes for making these adults, meaningfully literate should be given high priority, so that the efforts of the Human Development Resources for their children are not adversely affected.

Thus from the above discussion it may be concluded that SAARC has not nationalised significant success. This would surprise or frustrate only those who expect too much in too little time.

SAARC can not be viewed as the Panacea to all the problems that South Asian countries have accumulated for themselves over the decades. Collective economic benefits has been the main rationale, as well as the drive behind SAARC. The scope for co-operation under SAARC is wide provided due care is taken to expand the interaction among different sections of the people on a large scale. Only the meetings of intellectuals, personocrate and artists will not deliver goods. It

Some of the Basic Social Services with Reference to SAARC Countries

Sl. No. Country	Bank	GNP per capita US $ 1992	Human Development Index 1992	Agri. as % of GDP 1992	Ind. as % of GDP 1992	Service as % of GDP 1992	Estimated population (millions 1992)	Annual population growth rate (%) 1960-92	Population Health services (%) 1988-95	With safe water (%) 1988-95	Access to Sanitation (%) 1988-93	Population per doctor 1991	Daily calorie supply per capita 1992	Life expectancy at birth (yrs.) 1992	Adult literacy rate (%) 1992
1. Bangladesh	146	220	.364	34	17	49	112.7	2.5	45	.84	31	12500	2019	55.6	36.4
2. Bhutan	160	170	.305	42	27	31	1.6	1.9	65	34	13	11111	—	50.7	39.2
3. India	134	310	.459	32	27	40	884.4	2.2	85	79	27	2439	2395	60.4	49.9
4. Malawai	157	230	.330	28	22	50	10.2	3.4	80	56	60	50000	1827	45.6	53.9
5. Nepal	151	170	.343	52	18	30	20.3	2.4	—	42	6	16667	1957	53.5	25.6
6. Pakistan	128	420	.483	27	27	46	129.3	3.0	55	68	38	2000	2376	61.5	35.7
7. Sri Lanka	97	560	.704	26	25	49	17.7	1.8	93	60	50	7143	2275	71.9	89.3
8. All Developing Countries	—	982	.570	19	34	47	4420T	2.3	—	1290T	—	—	2546	63.2	68.4
9. Least Developed Countries	—	213	.337	42	16	42	540T	2.6	260T	280T	340T	18654	2027	51.4	46.5
10. Sub-Saharan Africa	—	559	.389	23	33	44	510T	2.8	200T	270T	290T	18480	2096	51.3	54.4
11. Industrial Countries	—	16054	.916	—	—	—	1200T	2.8	—	—	—	—	—	74.4	—
12. World	—	4534	.759	—	—	—	5420T	1.9	—	—	—	—	—	65.7	—

Source: Human Development Report, 1995.

is the common people of these countries, who can keep the SAARC ship moving. For instance, we have organised tourism within the region on a large scale, greater frequency of inter-country competitions, provision of a large number of scholarships to students for studies in a neighbouring country etc. Thus, SAARC can only succeed to the extent the peoples of the region patronise it.

References

Human Development Report (1995), UNDP, New Delhi.

Dala, K.L., (1991), Human Development and Indian Perspective, Har-Anand Publications, New Delhi.

Nasir, Naquash, (1994), SAARC: Challenges and Opportunities, Ashish Publishing House, New Delhi.

Pandey, B.N., (1980), South and East Asia, 1945-79: Problems and Politics, The MacMillan Press Ltd., New York.

Sudhakar, S., (1994), SAARC: Origin, Growth and Future, Gyan Publishing House, New Delhi.

Services and Development Potential: The Indian Context, (Papers from the UNCTAD/ICRISR Seminar).

Baugh, W.E., (1977), Introduction to the Social Services, The Macmillan Press Ltd., New York.

12

Duality and Growing Inequity in Social Sector Development

S.J. SRIVASTAVA*

Growth of Social Sector occupies a place of paramount importance in the process of economic development. The entire socio-economic framework of a country is directly or indirectly affected by its shape and size and its importance cannot be undermined at any stage of development. Social sector is primarily concerned with a sustainable increase in the access to basic essentials of life. A gradual expansion of these essentials contributes much to bringing about quantitative and qualitative change in the economic status of the people. In short, Social Sector Development is a key factor in the process of economic development.

More than half a century ago we solemnly resolved to constitute India into a Sovereign Democratic Republic and promised all citizens social, economic and political justice and liberty of thought and expression, belief, faith and worship and equality of status and opportunity. In the light of this commitment the development of Social Sector deserves our serious concern both in bureaucratic and political set up. We as

* Senior Lecturer, Department of Economics, D.B.S. College, Kanpur.

conscious citizens of this large democracy are supposed to keep abreast of the policy changes made from time to time. It is sad to note that during the last few years a wave of social discontent has set in and social sector development is suffering from serious setbacks. Duality and inequity have become its hallmark. The common man in the country keeps groaning under this reckless and ruthless machinery which compels him to accept an unbearable economic cost as and when he decides to avail health and education services. The recent wave of Privatisation, Liberalization and Globalization has brought about a drastic change in the attitude of the custodians of our welfare. Now they express great anxiety and serious concern about the increasing fiscal deficit and readily agree to all such proposals that may somehow mitigate government expenditure. As a result of this change in the attitude of the policy-makers there has been a phenomenal growth of Public Schools and Private Nursing Homes throughout the country. That way, Social Sector has definitely shown an appreciable growth but it has by-passed the interest of the common man. The fact is that the common man is denied the social opportunity for human development which is his constitutional claim and a fundamental right. In the name of Economic Reforms if we give a free hand to private institutions in the name of quality education and advanced medical facilities it augrs ill for our democratic values and makes our government answerable to the constitutional guarantee of social, economic and political justice. The moot point is—should we accept this change silently or make a protest against it as it touches the interest of already working institutions under government ownership and control as well as the growing class of people who fall either in the category of the people below poverty line and the middle income group. From the ethical point of view governance and commerce are two different lines of business and they cannot be equated on the basis of the cost of the service and its returns or productivity. The balance sheet of the state is naturally different from that of a corporate unit. The state machinery is always supposed to extend its area of production and distribution of all essential goods and services without giving any importance to returns thereof. The state machinery works with the motive of assuring social, economic and political justice to the poor and the deprived.

It is a known fact that after Independence Social Sector (with special reference to Health and Education) grew in our country under the government care and ownership. Even now the area of Health and Education is fairly large and more than half of our population consumes these services produced by government units. Any shrinkage in their funding or an indifference to the deterioration in their quality means affecting economic welfare of the masses. Inviting private institutions in this area of economic activity obviously exposes government's incapability to control the declining efficiency of government aided schools and colleges as well as hospitals. Likewise it also exposes government's failure to curb effectively the corruption related to productivity and misappropriation of funds. It is difficult to believe that government equipped with sovereignty can ever be so helpless and inert unless men in the government are themselves partners in this sordid drama.

With a view to serving the people and enabling them to exploit their latent potentials, government's interference seems to be the first desirability. The state should never feel reluctant to accept an increasing expenditure on Health and Education services as that is invariably productive. It is a step forward in the making of an egalitarian society. Increasing expenditure in Social Sector means designing more and more suitable policies to upgrade the quality of life of the millions of the people who form the core of Indian Democracy.

We must appreciate the visionary quality of our leaders who at the dawn of Independence realized it well that continuous growth with self-reliance was a difficult goal to achieve and it would remain a far-fetched reality until people from all walks of life are given an opportunity to contribute their all to the process of nation building. In fact, here lies the genesis of our concept of social sector and also its development. We deliberately chose the development of Social Sector under government care and nurturing so that personal vices like greed of money and lust for power might not enter into the realm of Social Sector service and it might function either with a missionary zeal or with obligatory duties to citizens. But to our dismay a sizable number of Public Schools and Private Nursing Homes have come up and local administration as well as the polity is giving them a green signal to function in their own way and with their own means. We have every reason to question the validity of such a policy that appears to justify market-friendly structure in health and education services. If services like health and education are made saleable and quality service is available when one pays a higher price for it, Society is pushed towards dehumanization process where members of the society are inferior and superior not because of any natural distinction but because of privilege and deprivation.

Government activities over the last few decades have all contributed to the burgeoning of the middle class, and this neo-middle class, in a bid to climb the social ladder, are desperately looking upon Public Schools as a tool for their children. The need of the hour is to appreciate this psychology of the middle class who innocently contribute to economic offences and help generating black money. This trend is disastrous. Let us pledge that we shall not encourage a system that divides our society into two classes—the Elites and the Deprived. Let our government come forward with firmness and see that duality and inequity at least in case of human development opportunities are eliminated at the earliest.

Let Indian economic development be more meaningful to the teeming millions before we step into the age of millennium. May good sense prevail upon men in Politics and Bureaucracy and together they appreciate the disastrous consequence of a sick Social Sector and revamp the existing system where the rule of man in the city of God could be justified and we may project a stronger India in the 21st century.

13

Development of Human Resources and Social Sector Planning

V.P. Tripathi* and Virendra Prakash**

Human Resource Development is now world over recognised as one of most important aspects of any development policy. Whether one is a developed country or a developing one, the need and importance of human resource development can not be undermined. While underdeveloped countries require development of human resource to intensively or economically utilise and develop their unexploited resources, developed countries have to develop the same to cater the need of their industries which undergo fast changes in technology and product designs so that they can stand firmly in highly competitive markets and withstand the jerks of cyclical economic fluctuations. Yet one can not deny that human resource development is much greater a problem in developing countries than in developed ones.

In developing countries with a abundant physical resources, developing human resources is not just vital but a pre-condition for the development. But developing human

* Reader in Economics, R.B.S. College, Agra.

** Asstt. Professor in Economics, Government Post-Graduate College, Morena.

resources in these countries is not an easy task. In fact, in such countries human resources suffer from multi-dimensional problems which may take a much longer time and a huge financial resources to get over. In this short article, we will discuss some of these problems in a broad framework. Obviously in the course of discussion our focus will be India in particular.

QUANTITY VERSUS QUALITY

The basic problem in the context of human resource development in our country has two aspects viz. quantitative aspect and qualitative aspect. In India, quantity-wise human resource is in surplus while quality-wise the same is in great deficit. This is quite obvious also i.e. when quantity of human resource is in much surplus (i.e. quite unmanageable). Its quality is bound to be inferior. Likewise, if quality is low, maintaining quantity at an ideal or optimum level is also very difficult.

Those who are even little aware of quantitatively swelling up and qualitatively deteriorating human resource problem of India how it quite well that how dangerous turn our 'Human Resource Problem' has taken. Presently, India is adding in a decade, more than the total population of Brazil which has an area two and half times more than that of India. In a single year, India adds more people than the whole Australian continent, which is much bigger in area than our country. This enormous explosion of human resource has made whole planning a failure.

During last fifty years of planning there has not been significant rise in quality of human produce. Inspite of the fact that there has been sizeable investment in developing human resource through training, career development planning etc. But all these efforts and investment could not borne much fruits. Not only that but whatever has been little improvement in the form of creating better skilled personnels, that too has been negated in the phase of deterioration in yet more important characteristics of human resource, i.e. moral values, discipline, work ethics, austerity and patriotism.

FAILURE OF HUMAN RESOURCE PLANNING

An enormous rise in quantity and sharp decline in quality of human resource shows nothing but utter and awesome failure of human resource planning, a part of Indian system of planning. In the history of Indian Planning if there has been a greatest failure on any front, then there is none but the human resource management. In last fifty years of planning, human resources problem has brought to fore many serious bottlenecks in the path of economic development. These bottlenecks are as follows:

EMPLOYMENT GENERATION

There has been chronic problem of unemployment encircling almost all the organs of the society. Indian society has been suffering from all kinds of unemployments, viz. full unemployment, under-employment, disguised unemployment, technological unemployment, frictional unemployment, cyclical unemployment, etc. Not only that but all the sections, e.g. rural-urban, skill-unskilled, literate-illiterate, graudate-non-graduate all sections suffer from the problem of unemployment.

The problem of unemployment is alarming even today after almost five decades of planning. The problem of unemployment still occupies the top most position among all other problems associated with social sector. The facts reveal that the average annual growth rate of overall employment (In both organised and unorganised sectors) declined continuously from 2.75 per cent in period 1972-78 to 1.77 per cent in 1983-88 but increased to 2.37 per cent in 1987-94. While there has been significant improvement in the growth rate in organised employment in the private sector from 0.43 per cent in 1983-88 to 1.18 per cent in 1987-94. For the first time the growth rate in employment in organised private sector exceeded the employment growth rate in the public sector.

Government has taken several steps to tackle the problem of unemployment in both rural and urban sectors. Yet the same has not been solved fully. The planning commission has prepared estimate of unemployment using data provided by NSS Organisation which may be given as follows:

Estimate of Unemployment as on April 1, 1990[1]

(In Million)

	Male	*Female*	*Total*
1. By Usual Principal Status (UPS)			
Rural	4.97	2.66	7.63
Urban	4.16	1.30	5.46
Total	9.13	3.96	13.09
2. By Current Weekly Status (CWS)			
Rural	7.06	2.92	9.98
Urban	4.59	1.31	5.90
Total	11.65	4.23	15.88
3. By Current Daily Status (CDS)			
Rural	7.75	4.59	12.34
Urban	5.91	1.66	7.57
Total	13.66	6.25	19.90

On the basis of the NSS data, 16 million persons can be considered as unemployed in the sense of 'Open Unemployment' in the beginning of 1990. On the basis of data obtained from previous NSS Surveys, around 12 million persons are estimated to be severely underemployed in the beginning of 1990. The backlog of unemployment for planning process could thus be around 28 million in the beginning of the 8th Plan. The net addition to the labour force during 1990-95 is expected to be 37 million. Thus the total number of persons requiring employment during Eighth Plan would be around 65 million. It is further expected that by year 2000 AD, the labour force will increase by another 41 million people. Thus by year 2000 AD, the total number of job seekers would be around 106 million. This would necessitate around 4 per cent growth rate in employment generation. This target seems to be unrealisable looking at the pace of employment generation in present time.

While the problem of unemployment remains to be quite serious from the quantitative aspect it is further accentuated when he consider the qualitative aspect. The policy of liberalisation on economic front bringing foreign capital and technology at our door steps has thrown many new challenges before the planners and policy-makers. Till now we had to worry only about the quantity the aspects of the employment now will have to seriously think of the qualitative aspect also.

The approach paper to the 9th Plan placed before the NDC has outlined the employment perspective as under: "Certain changes in the structure of employment and unemployment between 1987-88 and 1993-94 need to be noted the rate of growth of female employment declined and this decline was particularly pronounced in rural areas. Further the rate of growth in employment in rural areas for both male and female during this period was significantly lower as compared to the urban areas".

Infact looking at the unemployment scenario, the problem is of multi-dimension as mentioned above. Therefore, to tackle it, it would be necessary, to adopt a strategy which is both suitable and feasible. Failure in this front will have serious repercussions on the social development. The problem therefore serious attention from both planners and policy-makers to provide people justice with equity, socially and economically.

HEALTH AND EDUCATION

(a) Health

The most important areas of HRD have been health and education, both these aspects deal with the quality in HRD. Health and education are complimentary upto some extent. Improvement in educational standard increases awakening among the people towards benefits of better health. People learn more about health hazards and thus reduces the incidence of diseases in general and epidemics in particular. Health education, therefore in a part and parcel of educational curriculum. Government has done a lot to improve the health standard of the people. There is decline of death rate in all the categories the life expectancy has risen to an acceptable level. Inspite of all this there are considerable regional variation thus there are considerable regional variation in health status in India. In 1996, for instance, the Infant Mortality Rate (IMR) varied from a low of 13 in Kerala to a high of 97 in M.P. and 95 in

Orissa. Similarly the life expectancy at birth ranged from a high of 72 in Kerala to low of 54 years in M.P. The IMR for rural areas was 87 whereas it was only 53 in urban areas.

Diversity in health standards in our country has been a matter of concern for our planners and policy-makers. Government has taken the problem of health on priority in the planning strategy. Being signatory to 'Alma Ata' declaration of 1978, government is committed to attain "health for all" by year 2000 AD. The strategy adopted by government on this front asks for promotive, preventive, curative and rehabilitative actions. Though health is a state subject, but Central Government is also playing a vital role in the improvement of health standard of the people. It has launched various health programmes on leprosy, polio, Aids, and other communicative and non-communicative diseases. Inspite of all these efforts by the government health conditions in the slums of cities and remote rural areas remains to be pathetic. A lot is still required to be done in this sector to provide the people minimum health standard.

(b) Literacy and Education

The importance of literacy and education as a tool of socio-economic change is well stressed by both social scientist and policy-makers. The level of literacy and education is directly related to the level of information and knowledge in society. These are the keys to the human resource development. The sustainability of economic growth and development much depends upon the growth of literacy and educational standards of the people. The level of literacy in India has been very low. According to 1991 census the level of literacy in India was 52.21 per cent. There has been wide gap between male and female literacy. Similarly, there is significant gap between rural and urban literacy accompanied by regional diversity. All this requires serious attention of the planners and policy-makers to draft and adopt a suitable strategy to tackle the problem of illiteracy. Several steps have been initiated by government to enhance the level of literacy and education among people. National policy on education, National Literacy Mission, District Primary Education Programme (DPEP), operation black board and non-formal education, etc. are some of important programmes started by government. Many International agencies such has World Bank, European Commission etc. are extending financial aid to tackle this problem. Government intends to increase the expenditure on education from present level of 3 per cent to 6 per cent. Inspite of all these efforts the level of literacy and standard of education in India is very low. This is the biggest hurdle in the path of developmental process of the economy. There is need to develop such programmes which have people participation as an essential elements.

Though these problems as discussed above are economic in nature, but they have social and political implications and dimensions as well. Their repercussions were explicitly observed during the recent reservation controversy and political instability. These developments clearly indicate that if human resource is not managed, our whole socio-economic and political fabric may come to threadbare.

Where Went Wrong

Although Directive Principles of state policy of our constitution included 'the right to adequate means of livelihood yet sufficient attention was not given to human aspect in our planning. As a matter of fact, the whole range of Indian planning remained basically production or growth-oriented rather than HRD-oriented. This is the reason why growth became focal point in Indian Planning and man was pushed to back-seat.

This seems to be bit strange that although first TYP was defined at correcting imbalances yet the same may be credited with starting a number of labour intensive industries such as Khadi and Village Industry Board, Handloom Board, Handicraft Board, Small Scale Industry Board and National Industries Corporation, etc. But successive plans and industrial and agricultural policies gave more and more emphasis on production, modernisation and technological development rather bringing human resource development on centre-stage. After 1970s some special employment-oriented schemes, namely NREP, Antyodaya were launched, but they too were neither comprehensive nor integrated with whole development planning. Obviously such isolatory approaches had little chances to make much headway.

Things were yet more deteriorated because on the one hand public sector could not generate employment potential of the economy, on the other 'Slogan of Socialism' killed entrepreneurship and hence depressed the self-employment opportunities. Indian planning created a misgiving that 'Government will herself do every thing'. Planning or leading role of Government never and nowhere means that state will directly put bread in every hungry mouth.

In essence, planning till 1980 failed to manage human resources productivity and in the best interest of the nation. After 1980 or so planning itself started losing ground and recently people as well as state is disillusioned with it. After 1990 the economic scenario has change of owing to new economic reforms. Planning, therefore, requires address to the issues which have come up due to economic reforms in HRD. Public sector alone can not take up the challenge on its own. The future of human resource development, therefore, lies in the hands of private sector. Recently we can see people specially the new generation more independent, more career minded and having less inhibitions in adopting any job or work. We are of the entrance 21st century. This is the age of information and technology. Now generation have to be well equiped to have their proper place in market economy. We hope this generation will read market requirements. We can therefore look forward a day when market mechanism and monetary motivations will successfully manage human resource development what planning system failed to do.

References

P.K. Bandyopadhyay, (1999), *Yojana*, Vol. 43 No. 1, pp. 73-75.

Dutta and Sundram (1998), Indian Economy, HRD, pp. 43-44.

Census 1991.

Planning Commission (1990), Employment: Past Trends and Prospects, 1990, p. 15.

Planning Commission Approach paper to 9th Plan (1997-2000), pp. 80-81.

Economic Survey, 1998-89, pp. 150-51.

14

Social Sector and Health Perspective—A Study

MUKULIKA HITKARI*

In this paper, an insighted attempt has been made to study the social sector in India with special context to health. A retrospective view towards the development approach, lacunae and achievements pointing to the growth process as well as malaise has been attained pointedly. The paper is categorised into five different sections. The first section deals with a brief introduction. The second section discusses an integrated approach of health with human and social development. An in-depth inter-comparative study of the aspect of health services in India has been undertaken in this core sector in the third section. In the fourth section, a short present health scenario in India has been attempted to be projected. Lastly, in the fifth section, certain conclusions have been arrived at alongwith various policy measures and suggestions being mentioned.

INTRODUCTION

Health—a significant welfare asset—has been argued to

* D.G.P.G. College, Kanpur.

be one of the major social inputs for sustaining a purposeful economic and an infrastructural growth. On the eve of five decades of independence, our government adopted a very surprising resolution on emforcing several policies pertaining specifically to minimum needs, health, nutrition, food, drinking water and sanitation as well as restraint of the unsustainable population growth perceived to be a commendable effort. However, the obstacles confronting their implementation need to be overcome. But the question arises is that, has a proper development strategy been formulated in this respect so as to impart an adequate treatment to the social sector?

Health can be credited to immensely contribute towards growth of social sector in India—if government gives way to required monetary allowances in its budget to this effect. But the Central government expenditure on health in 1991-95 was 2% of GNP (Gross National Product), whereas in nations like Ghana, Zambia and Sri Lanka—it was 7.8%, 9.9% and 5.5% respectively for the same period. Even after fifty years of independence, our government has played second fiddle to the social sector in India; thereby slashing its goal of equity and social justice. Despite subversive forces frustrating our efforts, we have repeatedly expressed and affirmed our faith and dedication for a broader outlook in well-defining this social sector—the spine of economic development.

Moreso, the status of health in developing countries like India (as compared to their developed counterparts) has forever been a victim of widening disparities. For instance, countries with low income have high health status e.g. Sri Lanka; while those with higher incomes have poor health status, e.g. Saudi Arabia. In recent times, the paradigm cannot be justifiably assumed that, by economic growth alone, the aggregate income and poverty levels could be improved. Undubiously, a broader consensus assumes that "Welfare" and "Equity" are the complementary variables enroute to gaining access to development strategies. As an imperative measure, the term development—in its reformulated form—verily entails "expanding crucially publicly funded social services."

HEALTH AND AN INTEGRATED APPROACH TO HUMAN AND SOCIAL DEVELOPMENT

The ultimate objective of all human endeavour is the attainment of happiness and welfare. Development demands commitment with a "human face". Efforts need to be largely concentrated upon the domestic front for redemption of the percent of population from bondage of poverty, uplifting living standards in terms of the availability of essentials of life, reducing unemployment levels, removing the system of concentration of economic power, overcoming regional disparities as well as improving the quality of human capital, both in terms of better health and education.

Our difficulties are complex in lieu of market-oriented economic policies which cannot adequately respond to the challenges of fundamental social issues in order to protect the interests of equity, social justice and harmony. A firm general impression which has gained ground, especially in the VII and VIII Plan periods, is that India's resolute commitment to welfare state as linked to social sector has been quite questionable. Obviously, market policies corresponding to welfare issues stand irreconciliable—thereby perpetuating social inequalities.

Human capital—a prerequisite to development in the social arena—assumes, vital significance in context of protection and its preservation. It can be stated that, as a matter of fact, human capital filters the developmental process into a performable one. Only this (human) resource covets an in-built mechanism in not only resisting but also combating the forces leading to exploitation in the social sector. Moreso, the phenomenal developments in the health services are quite deteriorating (e.g. mortality rate, accidents, drug abuse, declining quality of life and access to medical care). These need a thorough and intense monitoring of its investigative causes. It can be cited as an exemplary case, that the lacuna in health services is often revealed, since benefits to the doctors though being near to satisfactory, yet the loss to patients' treatment and care is still greater (not even marginal)—a said and justified cause of resentment in the have-nots circle.

Notably, the population-health syndrome has frustrated

our efforts at development innumerably. To add fuel to the fire managerial and administrative ineptitude plus fund misappropriation has projected itself in the sorry state of plight of patients in government hospitals—for urgent want of some life-saving treatment. Again, in the field of nutrition and health care, the repercussions should be felt both at the micro and macro levels. A sense of social capability ought to prevail where individual skills should interactively lead to enhancement of productivity. It should be remembered that the social factor would be offset by a weaker state of health potentiality. However, the constraints applied by income and poverty, too, severely limit human abilities. Thus the view that development of economic reforms manifests in social infrastructure proves its significance. To be ascertained, growth productivity increases the human capital consequent upon government programmes for reducing poverty level, income distribution and enrichment of social sector.

The United Nations Development Programme (UNDP) has with a firm conviction—focussed sustainedly on human development for social attainments and economic reforms with enhanced capabilities in the social sector since 1990s. In a parlance its the human capital which is to be made requisitely accessible. The UNDP's considerations imply that health sector plays an instrumental role in human development—thereby according greater heed to 'basic health services' instead of curative care for working population, i.e. "preventive measures", emphasisingly, be preferred to "curative methods". For example, in poverty ridden economies like South and South-East Asia — where health problems generally persist the calling need of time is adoption of a more holistic approach pertinent to health care. This accounts for higher nutrition, water supply, sanitation and housing conditions rather than merely placing medical treatment and care at the centre-stage.

Therefore, approach towards human development aspect desires its integration with social services provision, (particularly pubic services)—lending greater responsibility to this sector. The investment in this regard could be sustained over longer time period for realisation of actual benefits. Social security as per the ILO guidelines, encompasses two aspects viz., 'Protective measures' and 'Promotional measures'; where income and employment generation programmes occupy an important role to play alongwith conventional anti-poverty measures dealing with distress (e.g. old age, sickness, maternity, accident, etc.). Nevertheless, the two measures mentioned above would coordinatingly, improve the state of human capital; and perpetuate an egalitarian vision of society. According to UNDP's Human Development Index ('HDI') India ranks 135th among 174 nations according to latest estimates of 1996-97— explaining the prevailing scene of low level of human development.

Another stylized fact is that better health nutritional standards raise the returns to investment ranging from students to adults. Various poverty alleviation programmes result in feasible income levels—if properly implemented—which spins off higher nutrition health and productivity. The VIII Five Year Plan (1992-97) stated that social sector development is the government's primary responsibility especially in view of ongoing economic reforms. The moot question arising is that have the budgetary allocations in this respect been to the much desired extents?

According to the Human Resource Development Report (HRDR) 1990, the continuous persistence of socio-economic constraints should be stressingly removed by appropriate investment of expenditure in the social sector. Active co-operation of the people cannot be devoid of as far as human development remains the ultimate goal. Virtually for being a well balanced economic beneficiary, the country's social service sector has to be prioritisingly examined so as to perceptibly produce—as an output—a socially capable human capital for development. In a nutshell, it is actually the 'welfare' doctrine which should have a upper hand in governance of health services—thus displaying its role in a positive fashion.

INTER-COMPARATIVE STUDY OF HEALTH SERVICES

An elaborate analysis within the country brings to light the domineering aspect of inter-state disparity while rendering of the health services. Our investment incurred in the area of public health has been a meagre 1.7% as against the world average of 9%. This is because of sheer lack of health awareness and preventive measures. According to the UN Report, India alarmingly houses the largest HIV infected population—still expected to be growing at a rapid pace. These problems would not have accumulated in the social sector and welfare domain had the gigantic task of enforcement and implementation been decisively maintained.

As per the social services utilisation these should be targeted basically at the poor for ensuring outputs. The VIII Plan has laid down fundamental and preventive care in rural areas—necessarily for assuring a gross equitable distribution of public sector health opportunities. But—contrarily—in the modern health care system, private hospitals/nursing homes that too demanded by people) impart quicker and quality services—henceforth churning out a profitable investment. This urban trend generally subjects the rural primary health centres (PHCs) leading to high cost and pitiable condition of treatment. Concerning the rural area coverage only Tamil Nadu, Karnataka and Gujarat have been able to target their-health expenditure to certain compensatory levels. This rural urban cost structure owes itself to differences in expenditure disbursements and grants; free beds exceeding the number of paid ones; patients not being properly attended to; and crossing the strength limits in admitting the patients to hospitals.

A striking feature, also, is the gender disparity prominent in rural areas (as against urbanisation)— where females are still less attended to than males. This is in relevance to minimum needs (the only exception is the deviated West Bengal where hospitalisation facilities for both male and female are alike).

Apart from this, a parallel medical system openingly exists—with opening of private nursing homes for better and expensive treatment—has led to erosion of confidence in public health services as well as dismantling of public hospitals.

Nevertheless, the low income groups are persuasively lured to get themselves admitted into private hospitals (even though not indispensable) despite the fact that their life-time savings at times cross their means of livelihood. Such a state of affairs amply exposes the designs of the medical profession nefariously in the public hospitals in almost every district—where doctors draw their salary from the government but prefer to make their services readily available in private hospitals. Observing the same stand the overcrowded public hospitals at present have witnessed transfer of patients to private ones; leaving only the unaffordable ones to buy treatment involuntarily. In such circumstances, therefore, it becomes quite questionable as to how public health schemes can effectively respond to challenges of market economy accompanied by the commitment to social justice, equity and welfare.

A major constraint is that the share of social services in total government expenditure (e.g. in Punjab and Haryana) is quite low compared to other states. In other words, the low "social allocation ratios" are being slashed with every budget, moreso since 1990's. Contrastingly, Kerela tops in education and health attainments (gaining parity with middle nations) despite low levels of expenditure being incurred by the government. In Uttar Pradesh, failure is accounted for due to an iniquitous economic and fragmented social sense, which thwarts the effectiveness of governmental steps and initiatives undertaken—believed to be substantially inadequate. Therefore, human resource development is eventually consequent upon reforms enforced in the social sector—majority inclusive of health scenario.

Certain important estimates reveal the pre- and post-reform allocations covering the health perspective. This would enable us to make an inter-state comparative study and the role of the performance of Central and State Governments combinedly. The total budgetary expenditure excludes loans and advances). The above mentioned fact has been assessed by relating the per cent of expenditure allotted to health, i.e., MPSW (Medical Public Sanitation and Water Supply) proportionately to the total % of expenditure on social sector on an "average from 1987-91 and 1991-97.

	1987-'91	*1991-'95*
1. Total on Social Sector	25.34%	25.42%
2. MPSW	4.37%	4.15%

This table shows that in the second five year average, though the total outlay rose merely by 8%, yet per cent on health further declined from 4.37% only to 4.15%. The implication is the lack of provisioning and insignificant attitude towards such services. The outlay is deplorably low as compared to even less income countries like Thailand.

The major responsibility still rests on the states who promote the social sector by incurring almost 80% of the total budget outlay. So the actual burden of implementing and streamlining the in process inevitably should rest with the states with competence.

The figures show the low level of response in accomplishing their task.

	1987-'91	*1991-'95*
1. Average expenditure	43.01%	39.96%
2. MPSW	8.34%	7.28%

Considering the budgetary expenditure of only the Central Government the highlight is the excessively meagre amount incurred by it as is evident from the following data:

	1987-'91	*1991-'97*
1. Total Percent	11.38%	12.00%
2. MPSW	0.48%	0.57%

Here, the Central Government in this arena has yet to modify its policies to give them mass acceptability with effective repurcussions.

Giving a different nature to inter-comparative analysis, the following information is obtained on dividing the country into six regions.

	% of expenditure averaging from 1986-'91	*% of expenditure averaging from 1991-'96*
Northern	5.42	4.81
Southern	5.99	5.34

Eastern	6.18	5.87
Western	5.03	4.43
Central	6.08	5.11
Nothern-Eastern	5.29	5.13

Notably, the percentage of allocated expenditure declined to a considerable extent in Eastern and Central regions; with the others equally registering decline but with lesser intensity. The expenditure for the Northern-Eastern region was already the least among others compared in the first half average and further decreased with the second average from 1991-96.

If we proceed State-wise on an individual basis, it is distinct from the figure—chart below—that the first five states ranking respectively in terms of allocation on health in the first half have all gone down in expenditure allocations in the second average.

	1986-'91	*1991-'96*
Mizoram	9.65%	4.23%
Goa	7.87%	7.30%
West Bengal	7.64%	6.34%
Kerala	7.39%	6.41%
U.P.	6. 53%	5.21%

The situation at loss' ordinarily, in the second half average period could still be explained to its minimum but for Mizoram which drastically curtailed its allotment (by 5.42%)—a massive amount which is quite perplexing.

Now, switching over to inter-state findings, several notified facts have indicated that:

(a) In developed states, it is the private hospitals where highest proportion of deliveries take place whereas in lesser developed states, these occur in public hospitals.

(b) Urban mothers are attended to carefully in private clinics under PNR (Pre-Natal Registration) for better health safeguards. But in well off states like Gujarat, Maharashtra, Tamil Nadu and Punjab, even 'rural'

PNR is still made with lady health visitors—with less care.

(c) Kerala bags the opportunity of ranking highest in rural births (78%)—with half of these occurring in public hospitals. This manifests itself in the conclusion that only Kerala can boost of a proportionate urban and rural development in health opportunities at relatively lowest cost; sometimes followed by states like TN, AP and Karnataka.

The World Bank Report, 1996 highlights the miserable health status stage in India as given below:

(i) Female deaths are relatively high in ratio to that of males upto 30 years of age;

(ii) Bihar, U.P., M.P. and Rajasthan account for 50% of infant deaths (out of 47% of births annually);

(iii) 63% children are prey to malnutrition and under nourishment;

(iv) About 1,50,000 women die during pregnancy or child births due to awful medical treatment effected to them;

(v) Number of maternity deaths in rural areas are among the world's highest.

To conclude, if the states per capita income is high, this alone does not obviate the need for protecting the poorer sections and social attainments can be achieved through specific area-based programmes of diffusion of PHCs. Likewise it would eradicate the concept of gender disparity to some extent— where women become victims of untreated ailments on a large scale. Though urban poor are placed favourably over rural poor, yet their condition is equally pitiable. This calls for two significant suggestions, namely:

First, subsidised health care facilities be provided and expanded; and

Secondly, some basic health services be freely supplied, including free beds—with no place accorded to the plea of resource crunch if it becomes an excuse for inefficient working.

PRESENT HEALTH SCENARIO IN INDIA

According to Art. 47:

"The state shall regard the raising of the level of nutrition and the improvement of Public health as among its primary duties.

But the truism is a failure by India's embarking in discharge of its primary duties. Even a cursory view would prove the reverse situation.

India has a few dubious 'highest' to its credit, viz.,

(i) Highest number of TB Patients in the world;

(ii) Highest malaria deaths;

(iii) Highest number of blind people;

(iv) Highest HIV-positive cases;

(v) Highest numbers of occupational casualties;

(vi) Highest numbers of hepatitis B patients;

(vii) Highest infant mortality rates; and

(viii) Highest incidences of malnutrition.

The major implementation of health services rests with state governments but, unfavourably, the 'State Health Programmes reveal a dismal performance picture. Our immunisation schemes cover only 70% (with misplaced stress on sterilisation and family planning) whereas population has doubled from 1976 to 1996.

The chart below shows the three worst states as compared to Kerala:

States	*Infant Mortality rate (1000)*	*Life Expectancy (years)*	*Primary Health Centre Shortfall*
Madhya Pradesh	106	53.4	644
Orissa	110	54.3	288
Uttar Pradesh	94	53.4	669

The following deplorable state of health care needs no mention when it is assessed in stark contrast to Kerala (topping in health care) where infant mortality rate is in ratio of only 12 to 1000 persons while the life expectancy is to a good 70 years.

The sketch of health care scenario would be incomplete without the case of the district " Tikamgarh" in Madhya Pradesh where more infant deaths occur than even in poorest Africa. For a 10 lakh population, only 23 PHCs function—of which 17 are manned only by a single doctor. The health centres are deserted generally; medicines are rarely available; growing pregnancy deaths; and patients unattended mostly are enough in explaining welfare conditions. Since 1980's the Health Ministry does supply medicines to districts to tune of Rs. 2000 but State Governments, as a wonder, hardly strive to increase their health budgets. Damningly, funds for health services in First Plan were 3% which whittled down to 1.05% in the Eighth Plan.

Thus, it is a paradox that despite some improvement in health infrastructure, it is the rural India which is deprived of basic facilities. It is estimated that there is one doctor for over 20000 people in various parts of the country while a chunk of health budget goes to urban hospitals at expense of PHCs in rural area—a case of misplaced priorities. Economists like Amartya Sen and Jean Dreze opine that even sub-Saharan Africa fares better than Tikamgarh. It is difficult for destitutes to pay even 50 paise for a single antibiotic tablet whose market cost varies from Rs. 7 to Rs. 10 per head. Hence a revolutionary awareness should be created for greater concern towards this sector and its channelised implementation.

CONCLUSION

The health status—gearing the social sector development needs to be studied comprehensively. Surveys as NCAER 1990 and NFHS (National Family Health Survey) 1992-93 created enormous awareness towards extensive utilisation of medical care. It is vital that realisation dawns timely on significance of this sector so that over-all economic development can become a desired process in the country.

An inescapable conclusion is the menace of rampant

corruption in dischargement of health services. As a matter of fact, the issue of health shouldn't be left merely at the mercy of market forces. Instead a dominant participation plus efficient regulation should serve as value-based and ethical guidelines for furtherance of cause.

This idealism involves high qualities of transparency, accountability, integrity, efficiency impartiality and human sense of work—where a candid attempt could result in their attainment. Moresoever, attention be paid to nexus among segments, of governance for, non-pretentiously, the existing quality deterioration in the area of health. Being a silent spectator to health abuses—leakage and misappropriation of funds despite availability—also proves a detriment to this sector i.e. it is unfortunate that tip of the iceberg is touched when health services are not effectively utilised. Therefore, the medical scenario reveals a picture of acquisition and agony as health services (its facilities financed by public resources) are most non-judiciously dispensed with—owing to privatisation of policies making this sphere comparably competitive.

In a nutshell—apart from the above endeavours—a more credible system has to be ensured so as to restore confidence of the people. A transparent and accountable system calls to overcome corruption and erosion of 'dualism' in public social services for rich and poor. Also, by a firm and apt managerial/ administrative sense, health status would be a welfare-oriented one with political intervention almost diminishing. Such a healthy spirit of competition would fulfil our perception of a just, equitous and egalitarian economy committed towards service.

Recently, Prof. Amartya Sen—the Nobel Laureate—for Economics and the first Asian in this field—won commendations for his intensive interactive study of economy going global sans social welfare. The persisting poverty and ill-health is quite devouring for the social sector—enabling the country to lose its standing significance in context of global market policies. Therefore, a "social safety net" has to be first laid down for an economy to establish its infrastructural stronghold—as a preceding factor to competition; or else the entire economic development would be a farce, without creation of social opportunities in an ample measure.

REFERENCES

United Nations Development Programme (UNDP) 1996: Human Development Report; Oxford University Press, New York.

Planning Commission (1991), Eighth Five Year Plan (1992-97); Vol. I, Government of India, New Delhi, p. 10.

RBI Bulletin Issues.

Issues of Central Government Budget Documents, Expenditure Budget, Vols. 1 and 2, Government of India, Ministry of Finance.

World Bank Report (1993): 'Human Development Resource Survey'.

'Healthcare', referred to in 'Outlook ', Oct. 19, 1998 Issue, p. 66.

Dr. Amartya Sen's article; 'The Times of India', Daily Newspaper, 16/10/98, p. 1.

Report of Economic Survey, 1996-97.

Indian Economic Association, 79th Annual Conference Volume, Gwalior, 1996; p. 253.

Government of India (1996); 'Health Information of India'; Ministry of Health and Family Welfare, New Delhi.

15

Social Sector Development and Economic Reforms

O.P. SHUKLA*

The new course which the Indian economy has taken since 1991 has significant implications for its social sector and for the vast numbers of people directly or indirectly for their livelihood. As is well known, social sector development encompasses all those sectors which contributes to an enhancement of human capital (Prabhu, 1996). Human Capital involves through education, in-service training, nutrition and health which leads to human resource development. The implementation of economic reforms has some diverse impact in enhancing people's capabilities. The accepted concept of human resource development is the 'Process of enlarging the range of people's choices' (UNDP, 1996).

However the present reforms are throwing this, sector open to the private sector.

Prof. Amartya Sen (1998) has emphasised the role of Public Policy in providing and expanding health care, family planning, educational facilities and other social security provisions. The

* Lecturer, Department of Economics, Armapore P.G. College, Kanpur.

characteristic feature of public policy in India is that it is more often inappropriate and inadequate. There is also no denying the fact that key to higher economic growth and development lies in improved situation of social sector. Thus, one of the major challenges in the coming new millenium is to prioritise social sector development quite equitably at the community level both in urban areas and in rural areas. Only then our economy can become a sound footing and strengthened. But inside this there is a genuine case for investment and fiscal prudence.

Since India being the second largest country in the world after China, it has been characterised as a country with a low level of human development with the country's rank in the Human Development Index (H.D.I.) calculated by the UNDP being 135 among 174 countries in 1996. At this level, the position of the country is lower than not only that of China and Sri Lanka but lower than that of Thailand and the Philippines which were in similar to India. In this context Individual indicators such as literacy and infant mortality in the country are also lower than the levels attained by other countries.

Some studies have indicated the weak links between economic growth and social sector development in India. Kerala having achieved high levels at human development but relatively modest economic growth rate. On the other hand, Punjab and Haryana which despite high levels of per capita income are substantially behind Kerala in terms of crucial social indicators.

Plan Documents have stated that social sector development is the primary responsibility of the government particularly in the context of the ongoing economic reforms (VIIIth Plan, 1992-97). Table 1 indicates the proportion of total budgetary expenditure devoted to the social sector as a whole increased from 24.43 per cent in 1991-92 to 26.76 per cent in 1994-95 whereas the same has decreased from 25.61 per cent in 1987-88 to 24.91 per cent in 1990-91.

Thus the table gives an idea about the priority given to social sector development in pre- and post-economic reforms. Also, at the micro-level individual proportions to various components of the social sector, a decline is found in all the

TABLE 1

Budgetary Expenditure of the Centre and All States on the Social Sector

Year	*Percentage of total expenditure*
1987-88	25.61
1991-92	24.43
1994-95	26.76

Source: Plan Document, GOI.

components except in the case of Education during the 1990-91 compared to 1987-88 (see various issues of Economic Survey). However on the other hand, an increase is found in all individual components (see notes) of the social sector except family welfare, Housing and Urban development during the year 1994-95 compared to the year 1991-92. Thus, on the basis of budgetary allocation prioritisation is revealed to social security and welfare and Rural development. Along with this there is an urgent need to step up the budgetary expenditure proportions to education, health and food security in order to promote human resource development. Also, there are glaring evidence of disparities in the expenditure pattern between central government and states on the social sector. Thus, inter-regional variations in terms of social indicators have emerged due to uneven spread of allocation of funds. (Sudhalear. and Moss, 1996).

Table 2 focuses on the quality of life that has been recognised (UNDP, 1997, NCAER, 1996). However Table 3 shows an enhanced human development expenditures particularly through education. An analysis of the budget of Centre and the State indicates that the expenditure on social sector as a proportion of G.D.P. have remained in the 90s at around 7.6 percent of the G.D.P. Expenditure in this context includes education, health, rural development and food security. Social services, i.e. education and health account for six percent of G.D.P.

TABLE 2

Disaggregated Human Development Indicators for India

States	*HDI value*[1]	*Literacy %*[2]
M.P.	0.341	46
U.P.	0.343	48
J.N.	0.432	52
Kerala	0.597	96
West Bengal	0.452	60
Haryana	0.476	56
Maharashtra	0.513	58
Punjab	0.516	60
India	0.436	58

Sources: 1. Haq, 1997.
2. NCAER, New Delhi, 1996.

TABLE 3

Percentage Expenditure on Education to Total Budgeted Expenditure

Year	*%age of total expenditure*
1951-52	7.92
1981-82	9.09
1987-88	11.27
1991-92	11.01
1996-97	11.23

Source: Financial Statistics (GOI), 1997-98.

CONCLUSION

Dreze and Sen (1995) stress that the strategy of development should emphasise on enhancement of human capabilities. In their view the success of any programmes cannot be judged in terms of their effects on income and output growth but on the lives that people can lead. In this aspect education and health can be important factors. Also expansion of health and education can have influences that go much beyond the immediate personal effects. The recent spurt of liberalisation and globalisatioon in our economy has rather necessitated for increasing attention to education and health because it will only be the manpower equipped with right knowledge who can dynamise the economy. Thus public policies even in the present era assume greater importance.

Financial stringency and international institutions conditionalities reflect in cutting public expenditure in the social sectors. Inadequate attention from the public side to this crucial social sector may block the economic progress with dangerous consequences. Thus one may say that any adverse effect of resource crunch on the social sector is bound to effect in turn the entire economy adversely. We need therefore to stress simultaneously economic development and social sector development to sustain developmental process in a more conventional source. To sustain this process in Post-reform period, both the government and the private sector, in a partnership style, are required to give attention to this sector of great relevance to economic development.

Notes and References

1. Individual components in the social sector broadly includes Education, Medical, Family Welfare1 Food Subsidy Social Security, Housing, Urban and Rural Development and Employment.
2. Total budgetary allocation excludes loans and advances.

References

Dreze, J. and A.K. Sen (1989), Hunger and Public action, Claredon Press, Oxford.

——, (1995); Indian Economic Development and Social Opportunity, OUP, Chennai.

Seeta, Prabhu K. (1996), "Social Sectors in Economic Development: Some Issues", Conference volume, 1996.

Sen, Amartya, (1998), "Hunger in the Modern World", Memorial lecture organised by F.C.I. to commemorate the Golden Jubilee of India's Independence.

Sudhakar S. and A.G. Mass (1996), "Government Budgetary experience on the social sector in India: Allocation Priorities, during the pre- and post-reform period", Paper presented in I.E.A., Annual Conference, 1996.

United Nations' Development Programmes (1996) : Human Development Report, O.U.P., New York.

Index